June

June

Tempered Steel

JUNE WHITHAM HOLROYD

iUniverse, Inc.
Bloomington

JUNE
TEMPERED STEEL

iUniverse books may be ordered through booksellers or by contacting:

iUniverse
1663 Liberty Drive
Bloomington, IN 47403
www.iuniverse.com
1-800-Authors (1-800-288-4677)

ISBN: 978-1-4620-5342-1 (sc)
ISBN: 978-1-4620-5344-5 (hc)
ISBN: 978-1-4620-5343-8 (ebk)

Printed in the United States of America

iUniverse rev. date: 11/22/2011

Starting again with life in England—August 1954

Our sail home from New York to England was pretty uneventful. We were on the new. *SS United States;* the ship was definitely more modern and comfortable than the old, *Europa*, and of course it was a pleasant way to travel to recover from all our crazy days, before we left New York. We changed the clocks one hour every night, so the jet lag problem, which you get when you fly, never existed. We only had to recover from the rocking sensation when we got off the boat in Southampton.

Mummy and Daddy and my little sister Elizabeth, had driven down to meet us, which was lovely. I remember I had a bright red, very full skirt on and was standing high up on the top deck, waving my skirt so that they were able to see us, and wave back. When we came alongside the dock we thought we must have a film star or royalty on board, as there were hordes of press waiting with cameras. Anyway we found out it was a Swedish chap who had gone to the States to have his sex changed into a woman. I don't know if he was the first ever, but there was certainly a huge crowd to meet him / her.

To go from Southampton to Sheffield in those days was a very cross-country drive, no fast roads or anything direct. Daddy had planned a picturesque route through the Cotswolds, we stayed in one of the prettiest Cotswold villages, Burford for the night. The road was so curvy with high hedges and narrow roads, and of course Daddy drove so fast, that it made Geoff feel ill again. He got out and walked for a while to get some fresh air. We hadn't been on anything but straight roads in the States.

We went up to my parents house on Dobcroft Road in Sheffield and stayed there for a while visiting Geoff's family and all our friends. We picked up our little new Morris minor with an open top, that I had ordered for us, while we were in Chicago, which was very exciting—to get our first car. Then we set out for the Lake District to stay with John and Kim Satchell in Kendal. They are our old friends from University days. After a few days John decided he would like to come with us to Scotland to the Edinburgh Festival. We had a lovely trip and saw some great plays, concerts and small late night reviews. They were putting on a Tattoo each night in Edinburgh Castle, which was all floodlit and looked great, with bagpipes echoing off the castle walls. Unfortunately the weather was very cold and the little hotel we stayed in was not centrally heated. After two years long stay in the heat in the US we really felt the change. The other odd thing was that when we came out of the plays at night, the whole town was closed; there was nowhere open to have a hot drink or snack. It was early days for the Festival, I am sure by now it will have places open after the shows. We took John back to the Lake District, and then went south to my parents.

We had asked our old friends Felix and Anthea, who were living on Chancery Lane, in London, if they could keep their ears open for a flat for us. Felix had been in the army with Geoff so we were very old friends. Here is a picture of Geoff in the Army Engineers.

When we were back in Sheffield we heard from them that Paul and Sylvia Poulsen, who had a lovely Georgian flat at 5 Great James Street, were leaving to move further out, as Sylvia was expecting her first baby.

Moving Back to London

We went quickly down to London, flats were very hard to find, as so much housing had been bombed and was still not rebuilt. Anyway we were lucky and got Paul and Sylvia's place. It consisted of a very large living room, with 3 huge Georgian windows, onto Great James Street, that went across the full front of the house, on the first floor, (second floor in the US.) The ground floor was offices for a perfume importer from Grasse in France. They imported all the aromatic flowers and herbs etc., to make the essences. It gave the building a lovely smell, especially when a new shipment arrived from Provence, and stood in the entry hall.

We painted our very big paneled living room in white and we put an anthracite stove in the fireplace, so we could keep it continually burning, as there was no central heating. We had a lovely gray carpet and some very thick black velvet curtains that Mummy gave us, over the whole window wall so it was always cosy. Next to the living room was the bedroom, and then the bathroom and kitchen beyond. It was perfect just what we needed. Our friends Peter and Alison Smithson, who were fellow architects from the North, (Alison was from Sheffield, but had gone to Newcastle to study architecture and met Peter there) lived on the next street to us, Doughty Street. Alison was expecting her first baby, Simon. Once he was born I was very near to do some babysitting for them.

It was lovely unpacking all our household things from our wedding presents and our Chester Square days, where we lived before we left for America. Chester Square was by then very expensive, George Weidenfeld had moved into Eaton Square and his parents Mr and Mrs Weidenfeld, who owned the house at 12 Chester Square, where we had had a flat, had no empty place. George moved them a little later to a house he bought on Sloane Street.

When we had arrived at my parents house I had written to the shipping people in New York to tell them that as it was entirely their fault, that our crates had been left behind in New York, as we had paid their bill in full, we expected them to send the crates by the next boat. Of course by then we had storage fees added, plus the items were no longer traveling with us, so we would owe shipping charges across the Atlantic. When we landed in Southampton I had gone to see the British Rail office, to tell them when our crates arrived to send them up to my parents address, I was expecting them to arrive on the next ship. Anyway I got a sheaf of correspondence back and forth and was about to get legal help on it, as on principle I refused to pay for someone else's error. (This was first apparent when we got onto the United States Liner, in New York to return to England, and found a letter from the shipping company in our cabin, after we had sailed, saying none of our shipment was on the boat, because when they had them crated, they were a little more weight than they had told me, and that I had paid for. This is at the end of my first book.)

One day a little British Rail truck arrived in London, and the funny little man had all our things! I couldn't believe it! We got bills for ages from the US but once we had everything I just ignored the bills, and for quite a long time they wrote in their letters that they would not release anything from the New York storage unless I paid them. I never found out how the things were released. I was able to write to them and tell them everything had arrived already and I had no intention of paying them.

It was great fun to be back in London, with all its bustle, and lively activities.

We were very near to Felix and Anthea, so we saw them a lot. Felix was working for the Evening News; he did all their theatre reviews and also wrote articles for them. He was always very amusing and witty. Anthea had her little boy Kent, who was born while we were in Chicago. We used to go down to Watermill House in Benenden in Kent with them. Felix's father, who had been an architect, had bought some old houses, years before, as he knew that underneath all the little lean-to's it was a Hall House from the 13th century, that had had small outbuildings added. He had worked for years restoring it back to its original form. He got every detail perfect.

Opposite was an old watermill, a three-story clapboard structure and a group of oast houses, the hop kilns have tall cone shaped roofs where the hops were dried before they were used for the local beers. He first converted the oast houses for himself and Mrs. Barker to live in. Then he spent something like 25 years to fix up the main house. It was really his life's work, and although it was pretty much complete, he did not want to move in, as I guess he realised it was the end of his big project. However one day in the winter he was ill in bed, in one of the oast houses so Felix got it organised to move everything over from the oast house to the beautiful main house.

It was such a wonderful place to visit. Geoff and I would go down with Felix and Anthea in Felix's old Riley convertible car, which was always open, even in very cold weather. Felix had some old flying jackets from the war (the crews all had to wear fur lined clothes, as there was no heat on the planes in those days) so we all wore one of those.

Our other old friends in London, John and Joy Brinkworth, had built a little house in Wadhurst down in Kent, and had left the Holland Park house, where Geoff had stayed with them before we were married. Geoff and John were also friends from the Army days, and the Theatre Corps. We also went down to Kent on weekends to visit them. John was still doing his portrait painting, and Joy was painting chairs and furniture with wonderful Dutch designs and making beautiful lampshades. She painted little rows of very quaint houses on the shades, and when you turned on the light the walls of the houses were all dark, but the little windows glowed with light and some rooms had silhouettes of people in the windows. She also created a lovely garden too in their house.

We started straight away to go again to the RIBA (Royal Institute of British architects) for lunches, to see all our old friends, and Geoff made contact again at the AA (Architectural Association) in Bedford Square, and we joined the ICA (Institute of Contemporary Arts) on Dover Street. It was at its liveliest then, with all kinds of discussions and debates, we met a whole group of interesting people involved in the arts.

Through the RIBA I found a job in Clifford Duke's office on Haverstock Hill in Hampstead. They were doing work in Africa again, a new post office and a hospital both in southern Rhodesia. It was not too huge an office; several of the people were from South Africa, working for a while in London to experience being based in Europe. We always had a lot of young people looking for work for a year or two in London, from New Zealand, and Australia as well as

South Africa. The same sort of thing we had just done in the USA. I think it is very important, for architects especially, to spend time in other cultures, so much to be learned from them.

The President of the AA mentioned to Architects Slater and Uren that Geoffrey had worked with Skidmore Owings and Merrill in the US, Geoff was asked to join their office as they had a client, Ivan Sanderson, who wanted a Lever House type of design for their new Sanderson showroom on Berners Street, they thought Geoff was right for the job; none of their office, had done anything like that before. In fact no glass curtain wall buildings like that had been built in England. It was a very exciting prospect and Geoff was very pleased to have such a great client as Ivan Sanderson and to have such an unusual building to design in London.

My old pal from Bents Green, David Allford from my first school, and 'holy bible' suitcase days I mentioned in my first book, and my first two years of architecture studies, had married Beryl Roebuck who had been studying languages at Sheffield University. Dave had got 2 years behind me as he had had to spend 2 years in the

RAF (Royal Air Force) and had been in India. When he graduated, they came down to London and he started to work at the well known architectural office of Yorke Rosenberg and Mardall. For a while they lived in a flat on Haverstock Hill, so we saw them quite a lot too, they visited us in Great James Street as we were so central, just near Holborn. In those days David and Beryl went round London on a motorbike. I remember Mummy who was staying with us, was very worried one foggy winters night when they left Great James Street, very late to go home. Not too long after this they bought a little house on Ham Common, an early 'Span' house. These were small modern terrace houses built after the war, we had a whole group of them in Blackheath, the area we moved to later, and also on the west side of London, in residential areas, they were a private development, and were bought by mainly young professional couples. Later Dave and Beryl outgrew that house and moved nearer in to the centre, to a larger house they bought in St. John's Wood.

David did incredibly well at Yorke Rosenberg and Mardall. He was given London's Gatwick airport to design, and did it so well that not too long after he was made a partner in the firm. He was always a very gregarious fellow and enjoyed all the wining and dining that is part of those big offices. They opened branches in Australia and Singapore, so he and Brian Henderson another young partner did a lot of traveling, and entertaining clients. They built the firm up to a huge size and built a very ritzy new office building for themselves, and then later built an even larger new office building. They finally made it a public company and sold stock in it on the market, before they retired.

I drove north to my office in Hampstead in my new little car. Luckily I was going the opposite direction to the crowds, as we lived in the centre. Geoff was so near to his office on Gower Street, so he was able to walk over.

I began to think about my plans for having children. I had always enjoyed them very much, their innocence and wide-eyed interest and enthusiasm for everything. I also felt it was a very important contribution to posterity, to leave some of our interests and talents to go on to the next generations.

Nowadays so many children are from broken families and suffer from parents who are selfish and not dependable. In today's world, the parents who are currently having many children are unfortunately from poor un-educated backgrounds. The countries with a high level of education are having fewer children and dwindling populations, which is very worrying.

In early March 1955 we discovered that I was pregnant. I was almost 30 and if I was planning a family we thought it was a good time, and as soon as we decided, I was very lucky and became pregnant. We were both excited. I didn't tell them in the office, as it was early days. However one morning the guy who worked next to me, one of the S. Africans (they were all white ones, and some were Afrikaans, and Dutch descent) came in late and said he had been to the doctors as he had a rash, but the doctor said don't bother about it, it was just German measles, the only people who should worry were people who were pregnant. I quickly hurried him out of our office, explaining that I was pregnant, so then all the office knew about it!

I decided to go to University College Hospital, which was near to us, and was well known for a really interesting doctor, Grantley Dick Reed. When I told him about the measles he said if I caught it they would abort the fetus. He was giving classes in natural childbirth, and then handling the pregnancy. He had written a new book, "Childbirth without Fear" which was very well known.

He had been a Doctor in Africa when he was young, and had been intrigued that the native women made no fuss about being pregnant, and when they went into labour, they would squat in a field where they were working, and have their baby on their own, and bundle it in a cloth on their backs and continue to work afterwards. On his return to England he was amazed that women had such a hard time with their labour. He thought it must be because they were so tense and afraid when they went into hospital, that none of the natural muscle movement to expel the baby could take place. Also muscles were flabby, compared with a woman who has done a lot of tough physical work.

There was also a lot of fear generated from the older generations, who talked of the terror, and women dying during childbirth. I think also it may have something to do with the crazy corsets women had squeezed into for years, to give themselves the wasp waists that had been so fashionable.

In our first class, which was also attended by husbands, he asked us to hold our arm muscles very tight, and he kept reminding us to keep the arm really stiff, and after a fairly short time we all felt real pain in the arm, plus the muscles were not free to work on their own. Geoff and I decided to do all his classes, and we really believed in his theories.

In September we went on holiday to Italy and Switzerland, it was lovely to be able to see lots of new places. Whilst we were staying on Lake Como, it was terribly hot, so I decided to stand deep in the lake to cool off. Suddenly I was aware of a hissing, just at the back of my leg, and it turned out to be a snake. We found from some people who were sitting near there, that the farmer who owned the field above the lake, had just cut the grass from the top of his field down towards the lake, so it was not a dangerous water snake. At that stage I knew nothing about snakes, we do not have them in England but it was scary enough to stop me going in the lake again. The interesting thing was that when my baby was born, she had a red birthmark just on top of her leg, at the same spot on my leg the snake had almost bitten me!

When we were waiting at the station for our return train, Geoff went off to get something, and I was left with the suitcases. Suddenly a train full of special needs children arrived on our platform, and I sat and watched the parents, so excited welcoming these children, a whole train full of them, and I was so shocked, it seemed like an omen, and I had never thought of the chance our baby may have some problem. When Geoffrey came back to me, I had tears rolling down my face! I had never been an emotional person like that.

I was very lucky as I felt great all the time and so kept working in the office until my last month of pregnancy, when my boss noticed I couldn't reach the top of my drawing board! My tummy wouldn't let me bend over so far. The only odd thing I remember was that I frequently was dying to eat some shrimp cocktail, so Geoffrey and I would go out and try to find somewhere serving it!

I think it was at the end of October that I left the office, and as my baby was not due for another month, I signed up for a typing course at Pittmans, as I had never had time to learn to type. Near the end of November, Geoff's Mother came to stay with us as she thought she could help Geoff look after the flat.

We went to the theatre the night before my baby was born, we were right up in the gods where the only seats were available as we just went at the last minute. When I woke the next day, Thursday November 24th I realised I was going into labour, and I also remembered it was Thanksgiving Day in the States!

I went into hospital about 10am and had a little girl, Sarah Marika Windle Holroyd about 2pm she was a good size baby, more than 10 lbs. I had a very easy time, Geoffrey was reminding me to do my relaxing breathing all the time. It really was a wonderful experience, I think I stayed in there for three or four days and Mummy came down to stay to help me into my new routine. Our pal from the Lake District, John Satchell came down to London then, I remember him coming in with Geoff as a nice surprise to see me in the hospital. Sarah was such a dear little baby and we were both so excited to be able to take her home with us, the beginning of a new family.

My brother David drove down from Sheffield after a week or two, and Sarah and I went up early for our Christmas visit, to stay with Mummy and Daddy. Geoffrey came up by train, just before Christmas and we were up at home for the holidays—a wonderful Christmas to be with all the family again.

How to Adapt to a New Life?

When all the excitement had died down, and we were back in London I began to feel very lost. I had never had a time when I was not working on or for some big project. No one had ever discussed the huge change in lifestyle for a career woman to suddenly be confined to the home with a new baby, that slept most of the time, and when she woke it was just to feed and go to sleep again. I was so used to going into the office and to the RIBA each day for lunch and meeting all our pals, and just having my freedom as I'd always had. There were currently, at that time, a series of letters in The Sunday Times from lots of women who had been lawyers, and doctors, some of them had got very severely depressed to the point of breakdowns and suicide. I was lucky that mine was not so bad, and of course the fact I had looked after Elisabeth (my baby sister who was born when I was at University) so much, fairly recently, gave me confidence in looking after Sarah. Since that time I have always tried to warn friends, especially if they have had a good career, and always worked, when they get their first baby, to be prepared for a real shock to your system. Geoff did not really understand what I was complaining about, he suggested bringing some of his drawings home for me to do for him. That was not what I was missing at all!

The other difficulty I had was that my Mother had very strong ideas about bringing up babies. She had been part of the Victorian ideas of rearing children. One of the things, which I didn't like, was that as soon as they were born, every time you fed them you immediately held them over a potty because it was supposed to be time for a bowel movement. I bought several books on child rearing, and the American, Doctor Spock certainly didn't think that was a good idea, he said the only person you train is yourself. I had memories of Elisabeth, my little sister, sitting on a potty for ages and pulling herself around the floor, not needing or intending to do anything.

The health visitor and the clinic we had to go to for weighing, vitamins and shots etc. thought that the new idea was to fairly quickly introduce solid foods. They had me start Sarah on cereals, and then every week to start a vegetable or the next week chicken broth. Mummy kept saying to me that it was a mistake, that <u>we</u> had only had breast milk for the first 9 months or year. Anyway poor little Sarah developed an allergy for one of the things I had started to give her. She could not even take breast milk and got so weak that even boiled water made her throw up. One afternoon she was so de-hydrated that she just lay there like she was dead, so I quickly took her round to Great Ormond Street Children's Hospital, as I couldn't think what to do next. They said I should give her salt in the boiled water. Later they conducted some tests on her sweat, and never found what she had been allergic to. Once you have anything like that happen, you don't know whose advice to follow.

For about 2 years she kept getting sickness attacks. At first they were every week or two, but gradually they got further apart, and finally stopped. Later in life Sarah discovered she was allergic to wheat.

When she was about 6 months old we went over on holiday to Holland to a wonderful house "T'Zod" over the water of the lake at Loosedrecht. The house belonged to our good friend Joy Brinkworth's Aunts, Tante Lot and Tante Reet. It was on stilts over the lake with boats moored underneath. The sound of water lapping on the boats was so restful. Tante Lot thought I should have Sarah on Buttermilk as she said it was great for stomachs. That was really my problem I did not believe anyone's ideas any more.

We did have a wonderful holiday there and that was what we needed, we went to Hilversum and saw Joy's relatives, and we went to Rotterdam and saw a very interesting architect there, Herman Haan, who took us to several of his buildings, and the new shopping centre. We went to his modern house. We also went to the famous Rietveld house near Utrecht, built in the 1920's, and Dudok's Town Hall in Hilversum. Holland is so small so we criss-crossed it several times. We had taken our little Morris Minor over on the ferry to Ostend, so we were very mobile. It was great to get to know Joy's Aunts, as we had heard so much about them. They each had wonderful elegant large old houses in Hilversum.

Joy had had an extraordinary life; she was the daughter of Eliot Makeham a well-known actor who was in many plays in London and several films. She had been brought up by these two Dutch sisters, who were very old friends of Joy's Mother. During the First World War in France they had all three been nurses Joy's mother from London, and they were from Holland. They had always remained great friends. When Joy was young she used to go over to stay in Hilversum with her Aunts in the summers. Her Father was always off touring with a play.

One summer her Mother sent her over there again, and Joy remembers waving goodbye to her, later that summer she was told her Mother had died of cancer. It must have been a terrible shock, Joy had not even been told her mother was ill. Tante Lot had agreed to bring Joy up in Holland, with her own boys, as Joy's Father was always traveling with the Theatre, and could not take care of a young girl.

When the Second World War started, the Germans occupied Holland, and so Tante Lot and her husband were worried as Joy was English, and the Germans were checking up on everyone living there. One day when Joy came in from school the Gestapo were there, waiting to arrest her, and she was sent to one of the infamous concentration camps for the duration of the war. Living was under horrendous conditions, and Joy says the boredom for all those years was terrible, as they provided nothing for them to do. When the war finished Joy was released from prison, and returned to England. She joined her father Eliot Makeham who was an actor in ENSA, which was an entertainment organisation for the allied troops abroad in Europe. When the fighting stopped they went over to Germany and they put on plays and entertainment. Geoff, and Felix Barker and John Brinkworth were all soldiers who once the fighting stopped, were moved into 30 corps, a theatrical production pool. That was how they had all met Joy. They were putting on entertainment for the allied troops.

After the war, Joy married John Brinkworth, who became a portrait painter, in London. Geoffrey had lived with them when he first came to work in London, before we were together.

Later Joy and John moved to Holland, where John got some great commissions to paint the Dutch Royal Family. He also painted lovely portraits of Mummy and Daddy, and a very sweet pastel of Elisabeth. He painted several portraits of me for our wedding present, but was never satisfied with them, so we never got one. We do have a very good pastel of Geoffrey that John did while they were in the army. Joy continued her wonderful folk art and raised two daughters. Even today I have one of her paintings on my bedroom wall, the colorful paint was thickly brushed over old wood planks she fastened together, it's beautiful.

Mummy and Daddy had decided to build a new house for themselves, all on one level, as poor Daddy was very lame still, from his injection in the war, and the stairs at night were very hard for him, and the driveway to the garage was incredibly steep at their old house. When it snowed in the winter it was impossible to get a car up. They bought a lovely flat piece of land at the end of High Wray Close, it backed onto Ecclesall Woods, in Sheffeild. The woods were very pretty to look into from the new property. It sloped gently down to the woods. They wanted Geoff and me to design their new house, so that was a good project for me. Daddy knew a contractor George Green, but he also knew some rather painful owners of a plumbing firm, who lived two doors away. They were determined to change several of our details, one of them was the box gutter we had designed. They said it only needed the regular half round cast-iron gutter, but in fact it was a huge roof, and their gutters were far too small, and never worked properly.

I had to go up to Sheffield for site visits, so would pile Sarah in the back of my little Morris. She had a Carry Cot and we used to have her in a little harness, on the back seat. If it wasn't raining I usually had the roof down, so Sarah always had little red cheeks.

John and Jano, our great friends in Chicago, had sent her a wonderful selection of clothes when she was born, so unusual for England. One outfit was like the flying jackets we wore in Felix's car, so when we had the top of the car open, she wore that and it was so cosy. We designed some lovely walnut furniture units that George Green made so beautifully, for the dining room, and for the master bedroom we used mahogany for the drawers and dressing table unit, and then a long headboard with 2 side tables for lamps on either side of the bed, all built in.

We had come back with some very different ideas from the normal little houses around. First the structure was very unusual they wanted to have a very large living room, and to have the whole wall facing into the woods to be able to be open, to slide away in the summer with no columns or supports so Daddy could sit and seem like he was outdoors. George was very keen to try to do the big span in pre-stressed concrete beams. We had a very heavy stone roof, which was required in that area, so pre-stressed beams were ideal. George made them on the site, and they have been perfect all these years. Any settling of the house would have prevented the heavy double glazed window wall from sliding away easily.

Mummy and Daddy were very thrilled with the new house and it seemed to be ideal for them. We got some wonderful publicity from it, as few houses in England were so carefully designed by architects, most were just builder built, to one of their old plans. Architectural Review did an article on it, and Nicholas Pevsner gave it high praise in his guidebook to that area.

We ourselves needed a new house, as the owners of our building did not like Sarah's pram in the hall downstairs, and there was nowhere to put her for some fresh air. I used to tie her pram outside to the iron railings in front of the house, and she would play with a toy and watch people go past. It was a very busy little street as we were just opposite Lincoln's Inn, the law courts. I would prepare a lovely healthy lunch for Sarah, but when I went down to bring her up to eat, I would find all kinds of chocolate wrappers in her pram. All the secretaries on their lunch break were feeding her some sweets, so she didn't want my healthy lunch!

We had some friends who had bought houses in a rather elegant four-storey terrace in Notting Hill Gate, and they were hoping to upgrade the rest of their terrace. One friend was Lawrence Alloway and his wife Sylvia, he was a well known art critic, and she was a painter, we knew them from the ICA (Institute of Contemporary Art) two doors away from them was another art critic from the Courtauld Institute. There was a house between them that was on the market. It had a very old couple, Theosophists renting the top 2 floors, and then one floor was vacant with lovely high rooms. The ground floor and semi-basement were occupied by a single woman. Housing was so short still, and the law did not allow you to give sitting tenants notice to leave, even if you were the new owner and needed their rooms. Anyway we took the chance on the old couple moving out, from the top two floors, as the lady was bed ridden, so we went ahead and bought it. I took Sarah over with lots of tins of paint every day and painted the whole of the empty first floor and all down the stairs. We got someone to paint the front of the house too, so it began to look very nice. We rented the first floor to a musician friend, as it was too small for us, then we waited until someone moved out. Anyway after a while, no one moved out, and as we really needed to move in to something bigger ourselves, we put the house back on the market for what we had paid for it. We got no offers and were wondering what was wrong. Then our real estate agent said people were suspicious as it was so cheap, he wanted to double the price. It sold almost immediately!

We then realised we needed to look a little further out, so I telephoned dozens of real estate offices, and picked one area one day and went to see all the houses in that area, that were in our price range. I had a friend on the next road to us, Dorothy. Her husband was an architect and they were welsh, their little girl Karen was about the same age as Sarah. Dorothy said she would like to come and look at houses with me, so we put the 2 girls in carry cots on the back seat, and took our lunches. Some places were so dismal we didn't need to even get out of the car to look. The real estate folk just gave you a bunch of keys that were tagged with the address and you went off on your own. We did Bayswater very thoroughly first, as Geoff would have liked that area, but there was nothing we could afford. We then went across the river and looked in Greenwich, Lewisham, Lee, and Blackheath. One Friday, late afternoon, our last stop when we were all tired, we stopped at a <u>huge house</u> in Blackheath. I couldn't believe my eyes, it was set back a long way from the road, and had all sorts of ugly little buildings in the front garden. Once you got through those the house itself was a classic and a National Historic Monument. Dating from around 1670 with long and short stonework on the corners and brick for the rest of the structure. It had keystone faces over every window and such elegant proportions.

It was very large, about 30 rooms on 4 floors. As we walked round poor Dorothy was getting more and more depressed by it, and I was getting more and more excited and convinced it was the house I really wanted. I was so thrilled I could hardly stand it!! When I got home I was raving about it to Geoff, and saying we must go down early the next day, Saturday, for him to see it. Next day we went off again, and Geoff was the same as Dotty, hated it and said 'Over my dead body' so I realised I had to think hard, how to change his mind, but I was determined to get it anyway.

A 17th Century Early Georgian Home

Spencer House
Greenwich, London, England

Offered by Gibb & Associates, Real Estate Consultants, Santa Barbara

I telephoned our friends Felix and Anthea, to ask them if they would like to go the next day, Sunday, to Greenwich for a lunch on the river, and I wanted to show them a great house. They were the perfect pair to have asked, both of them had fathers who were architects and they were both very knowledgeable about historic buildings. Off we went. We went first to the house as I still had the keys. The owner, who was an architect, had moved up north, as he was never able to get rid of his sitting tenants, and so he was not able to move in. He had advertised it that Sunday in the papers, as the tenants had left and he had come down from the north and was going to hold it open after lunch.

Felix and Anthea were wild with excitement the same as me; they thought it was such an amazing find. Felix said I must write a check for a deposit straight away and leave it with a note for the owner if he got there before us. We went down to one of the pubs on the river and had lunch, and then back to Spencer House, 23 Dartmouth Row, Blackheath SE10. I don't think Geoffrey and I had ever been to the area, though of course we knew the history of all the famous buildings on the river in near by Greenwich.

Greenwich was the original location of the Royal Palace. On the River Thames, and was built by Humphrey Duke of Gloucester in 1447, he named it Bella Court. Greenwich Palace was the principal royal palace and a favourite for Henry V111, to live. He was born there in 1491. Two of his daughters Queen Mary 1st, in February 1516 and Queen Elizabeth 1st, in 1533 were born there too. It remained the favorite palace for the next 200 years. Those were exiting times as the British Navy ruled the seas and had direct access to Greenwich on the River Thames.

Once we were residents there we realized that the area had many advantages, an incredible history and beautiful elegant houses from the same early period built by all the court and palace nobility. Greenwich Park and Blackheath at the top of the park is beautiful open ground. In England protected open spaces like these are preserved forever. In US it is almost impossible to protect any open space, greedy developers and speculators have free rein, which is a real tragedy.

Blackheath is downstream to the east of London, and is on the south side of the River Thames. Greenwich is on the river below, and the Heath is on the higher ground, above London and the river, with great views over the whole of London.

After lunch, as we waited to talk to the owner, other people were going from one big room to another, about thirty rooms on four floors, and they were laughing to think of their furniture in such big high rooms and such a huge house. I began to realise I was taking on a very large challenge, but it certainly looked worth it, and as I planned to be at home with children, I would make it my project for the next several years. It was a perfect time to create more places for people to live, as there was such a shortage of flats in London, and around Greenwich and Blackheath, so I knew there would always be a big demand for the three other floors and we would have the beautiful ground floor level (flat) with a big walled garden to live in. There would be a very good income from the three other flats, which I planned to use on all the work that needed to be done on such a beautiful old Historic Building. It took a week to hear our offer was accepted and six months later we had final ownership.

Spencer House

I need to give a little of the history of Spencer House at this stage, so you can understand my tremendous enthusiasm. The house, was built in 1670 by the Earl of Dartmouth. It was called Spencer House after the Prime Minister, Spencer Percival who had lived there for a short period and was later assassinated in the Houses of Parliament.

At that time the Royal Palace of Henry VIII was in Greenwich and many of his court had houses in the area. The Royal Land extended up through Greenwich Park and onto Blackheath, Spencer house was built on the King's property. The Earl of Dartmouth had a house next to ours that was built on Dartmouth's own land, in the Lewisham Borough. Next to his chapel he started to build our house, which it turned out was not on his land, but on the Royal Land, and in Greenwich. The Earl of Dartmouth was the First Lord of the Admiralty and was in command of the British Fleet, and perhaps he felt he could take such liberties, however he was involved in a disastrous sea battle and on his return to England, he was put into the Tower and the charge was he had stolen Royal Land. I guess they couldn't jail him for losing a battle. He died in the Tower, but his son, who was then a court favourite was later given the house back. I don't think he ever moved in himself. the house was occupied by nobility and finally the Dartmouth family sold it in the 1930's. A future Earl of Dartmouth was created Lord Lewisham and his wife, Lady Lewisham, is the stepmother of Lady Diana, Princess of Wales.

The house, was designed by Nicholas Hawksmoor, who worked in Greenwich with Sir Christopher Wren and Inigo Jones. Nicholas

Pevsner in his guide to London praises the architecture of the house, "But perhaps the finest houses of all are further round the heath, in Dartmouth Row. Spencer Perceval House was built towards the end of the 17th Century. The keystone faces, with classical masks are particularly fine. It is an unusually interesting Carolean building"

Blackheath, which is the open Heath behind the house, is elevated high above London with magnificent views, like Hampstead Heath in North London. It was originally a very wild place and cutting across the middle of the Heath was the old Roman road from London to Dover, the southern port that led the conquering Romans into London. Dartmouth Row runs at right angles to this old road. There were houses of the same period opposite ours and they were smaller, single family houses with interesting people living there whilst we were there. Lord Altringham was in one, he gave up his title to protest the Queen's dreary speeches and became John Grigg and his wife Patsy. They were wonderful neighbours.

The other houses had the editor of The Times in one, the editor of The Guardian in another, and a young couple called Blunt, he was the nephew of Sir Anthony Blunt who had been the keeper of the Queen's Paintings and disappeared to Russia.

Blackheath was the scene of many historic events. Members of visiting royalty from Europe were met on the edge of the Heath and escorted through the Royal Park on the wonderful tree lined entrance to the Palace on the river. Greenwich Park is the oldest of England's royal parks and runs uphill from the river to the Dover Rd. on Blackheath.

Two centuries later after the Civil War and the Restoration of the Monarchy, King Charles II commissioned Christopher Wren to build an Observatory at the top of the hill, away from the smoke and fog of London. In 1674 Charles II knew that the most perplexing problem for the great sea faring nations, was measuring longitude. Latitude was easy. The ancient Greeks, by measuring the angle of the sun, found it was possible to know how far north or south of the equator you were. The hope for latitude lay in astronomy. If they could map the movement of the Moon against the backdrop of the stars, navigators could use the heavens like a giant clock.

John Flamsteed was the first astronomer Royal in the new Observatory, with long telescopes and seven-foot quadrant, he was able to prove the earth moved at an even rate, and began mapping the heavens. In the next decades the astronomers made their start charts, but the navigation problem still remained, ships did not know how far East and West they were from land. In 1707 four Navy ships sank with a loss of 2,000 men when they ran into the shoals of the Scilley Isles. Parliament offered a prize, the equivalent of 33,000 US dollars to any one who could find a way of determining longitude at sea more accurately.

John Harrison, who was an uneducated son of a Lincolnshire village carpenter, spent the next 46 years before he came up with a pocket watch that could keep accurate time on a moving ship. All these devices solving the longitude problem can be seen in the Royal Observatory in Greenwich, which is now open to the public.

Blackheath, to the sportsmen the name suggests the oldest rugby football club in England, and a place where golf was first played—when King James the sixth of Scotland became James the first of England and came to live in the Tudor Palace in Greenwich, he introduced the game to his new subjects in 1608, golf was played on the Heath until 1918.

The area is the site of the rebellions of Wat Tyler in 1381 and Jack Cade in 1450. Henry V's Victorious army were welcomed and applauded there on the Heath when they returned from the Battle of Agincourt in France after thoroughly beating the French in 1415. On the Heath behind Spencer House, Henry the eighth welcomed the Emperor of Byzantium and the Emperor Charles V on their visit to the court in Greenwich. The Mayflower set sail from the Thames in Greenwich, for America, and most of the crew and captain are buried in the little churchyard in Rotherhithe, near by. A recently popular figure, Pocahontas (because of Disney's film about her) is buried near there too, in a church in Woolwich. She had come over as a young girl to speak to the King and government, to appeal for her native Indians in America, but whilst in London she had caught the plague, and died. Sailing down the Thames she was taken off the ship in Woolwich and buried there.

The whole of Spencer Perceval House was kept as one for 200 years, and when it was divided into two, the left hand side was called Perceval House. They inherited the grand stair hall, which occupies two whole bays, our Spencer House section had the Grand Salon or Ballroom. The house had been split in two in the late 19th century.

Just prior to our purchase two sisters had lived there, one had the first two floors, and the other the upper two. They had both been married to doctors, but were both widows. The poor architect who owned it before us, had hoped to move in to the house (just like our plan when we purchased the Notting Hill Gate house) but could not get the 2 old ladies out. He had decided to take a job up north and sell the house, but recently the old sisters had left. When we saw it, it was all empty and was in a very sad state. They had had a V-1 flying bomb land next to our house in the 2nd World War, (Blackheath area was very heavily hit) which had destroyed part of our cornice. One of the beautiful garden rooms had been used to store coal, they only had open fires, so it must have always been freezing. All the brickwork needed re-pointing. Spencer House is a Grade A star Historic Building, everything had to be done with approval, and nothing externally could be changed.

Sarah was just one year old when we put our offer in to buy it, but house purchases are incredibly slow in England it was not finally closed until early 1957. To get a loan then you had to agree to furnish the apartments, as if they were left empty you could get the dreaded 'sitting tenants', which meant the value of the house dropped a lot. Felix and Anthea had by then had a little girl Maxine, she was 6 months younger than Sarah, and so they were very cramped in the little Chancery Lane flat. They asked us to give them a 5 year lease on our first floor flat, which is actually the second floor level our flat was at the ground level, they said they would do all the fixing up of that floor. We decided to take the ground floor for ourselves as it opened onto a huge walled garden on the back of the house, the south side. That floor had 5 rooms and a kitchen and bath and a big entrance hall, and Felix's floor had the same.

I decided I needed an 'au pair' girl so I could get on with such a big project. A friend recommended a Spanish girl, Elena so we took her when we moved down there. I first worked on one smaller room at the front of the house, as our new living room, it had beautiful early Georgian paneling.

Which was always painted, so I painted that white, and we put a big gas fire in the fireplace so we could heat the room very quickly. We got a local contractor to rebuild the kitchen; it had had a pantry in it, and was just a small corridor when we got the house. I repainted a smaller room for Elena. Then we were ready to move from Great James St.

I made a list from the very beginning of what finally I needed to do, and put it in order of importance. I wanted to get the other 2 floors painted and rented, so I could use the income to spend on the house. The lower floor had the previous owner's mother there for 6 months, so I started on the top floor, up above the top cornice, I painted and furnished it and rented it to a teacher called Ann, she found 3 other girls to share it with her.

When we moved in to Spencer House I discovered that I was pregnant again, the baby was due in early November. I went to a very nice local Doctor, Howard Reeve, and he was a family doctor who treated everything. He gave me the name of a really good midwife, so I decided to get our big Ballroom done and have the baby in there.

Elena went back to Spain, and I decided that I would be better with Scandinavian girls or Dutch, as they lived a more modern way, like we did. Elena was good and useful but she was always trying to put Sarah into her pretty frilly dresses, and telling me that her sisters in Madrid had all white dresses for their children, and changed them 2 or 3 times a day. I wanted Sarah to be able to play in the garden with Felix and Anthea's children Kent and Maxine. Sarah always introduced Maxine as 'my best friend' and from the beginning they were a good pair together, Maxine was a sweet little thing.

We got a really great Finnish girl, Ennie Metsola, who I really loved, she was such a great temperament and always laughing. She had had a very sad little life, her father had had a drinking problem, he was apparently very sweet with Ennie and she loved him very much, but he had died when she was quite small, and her Mother had married a very religious nut, who was the opposite of her own Father. When Ennie was in her teens her Mother had gone in for tonsil surgery and had died under the anesthetic. Then her Step Father had married someone very like himself, up tight and a religious fanatic, so Ennie had moved in with her Granny. She had recently finished school and had come over to London to learn English.

The au-pair girls in those days were a wonderful institution; they were all newly out of school and wanting to learn English. Their parents could not afford to send them to school in England, and London was very expensive to have to pay for your keep. I always wrote to them before they came over, and explained just exactly what I expected them to do. There was a good language school, Goldsmiths College, near to us, It was free, so most of them went in the afternoons to a class, and we put a TV in their room so they could hear, and get used to all the different accents. I got a little notebook and each time I had to explain a new word, I asked them to write it down, and learn it, otherwise I had to keep telling them the same word over again. None of them left us without becoming very fluent in English.

They were like an older sister to the children, helped me in the morning to get breakfast, and get the children dressed. Then they did the breakfast dishes and picked up in the children's rooms. If I had to go out they would spend the morning watching or playing with the children, three or four afternoons they were free, and if Geoff and I were not going out they were free in the evenings too. I did not ask them to do any cleaning, as I had a wonderful cleaner, Mrs. Neville, who came to me for years. She loved the children and would come up and baby sit any time I needed her.

While I was working on the big ballroom, I had kept saying to Sarah 'I am getting this ready for the new baby.' One day I was up in town and Ennie was ironing in the nursery room, when I came back I said straight away, 'Where is Sarah' and Ennie had been happily working away, and not noticed that Sarah was not around. We went all round the garden and into the other rooms, except the big Ballroom one, that I was working on, and had kept the door closed, and she wasn't there, we thought she might have followed our rather stupid dog up the road, so Ennie went running off, when I heard a little noise in the BIG room (the old ballroom). I opened the door and there was Sarah with one of my cans of white paint which I had left out to get it finished, daubing it on the bed spread and all over the babies cot and lots of paint on the floor, and she said

'Ar paintin for baby' when Ennie came back she was laughing away at the awful mess. We had to get the bath filled with water quickly, before anything dried. Luckily they were all water based—paint, so washed off fairly easily!

Ennie's step-father sent her money every month as she had been left it from her own mother and father, each time it arrived she would go off into town and buy new shoes and take her friends out for coffee and cakes. Towards the end of each month she was always broke! One day the railway police arrived at the house and wanted to talk to Ennie but she was out, luckily, so I was asking them what was the problem and apparently she had changed the date on her monthly rail pass, extended it for another period. I explained to them her whole difficult life, and so they just agreed to give her a warning, not to try that again.

The funny thing of Ennie's shoes was they always had rather high heels and she walked in them in a sloppy sort of way and she was quite a heavy girl, after a very short time the heel of one shoe would break off. When she left us, her cupboard was full of shoes with no heels!

I spent all my pregnancy working very hard on the house. As the Mother of the previous owner had left the lower floor flat, we got builders in and did a new entrance at the side of the main steps, the new entrance went into two old vaulted wine cellars, one we made the entrance hall to that flat and the other we made into a second bathroom. We built a new kitchen off the living room and a new bathroom off the main bedroom.

About that time I was down visiting our old friends John and Joy in Wadhurst, Kent, with Sarah, and in a country antiques, I found a very simple, old, wrought iron gate, so I bought it and took it back to Spencer House propped up, in the back of my open car.

About the same time they were demolishing the old almshouses in Lewisham, and the bricks were from the same period as the ones on Spencer House, and their garden walls had a 'V' shaped capping on them, all in very nice old stone. I bought all the bricks and stone and had it delivered into the front garden of Spencer House.

The house had originally had a low 1ft. brick wall with stone coping and a cast iron railing on the top, but during the war everybody donated their iron railings for scrap, so they had been cut off. When we had lived in the house for a very short time, a little fellow from Lewisham Town Hall came, he saw I was doing work on the house, so straight away they increased our property tax rates! Although Spencer House was a listed Historic building, they gave you no encouragement to keep it in a good state, structurally. He said 'you know how I knew you were here, from the milk bottles delivered on your step.' (Like a bunch of spies) I put in a protest as it was such a highly prestigious listed building, and they needed it maintained. If we hadn't bought it and fixed it up, I can't imagine what would have happened to it.

Another man came from Lewisham Council and said all the strange little sheds and buildings in the front garden were on a special annual permit, built during the war for storage, and did I want to renew it, so I said 'no' and I walked along to the end of Dartmouth Row, to an ancient car repair place and borrowed a huge sledge hammer and knocked everything down. When Geoff came home he was very surprised, it looked like a bomb had hit all the brick sheds.

Now that I had my gate and knew what width to make the gateposts, I decided to build a high brick wall at the front of the house as newspapers blew in and dogs came in too. We also had some tour buses stopping to see the house, and everyone would get out and peer into our front rooms. We needed more privacy. During that summer of 1957, I found a very bright boy in Lewisham who had just left school, so he came up every day and mixed concrete for me, and I started on the wall. I didn't want it to look brand new with hard trowel joints, so doing it myself I ran my gloved thumb on each joint and it ended up looking like an old brick wall. I went to the local cemetery and got the stonecutters to do me a stone with 'Spencer House' on it and also cut two large stone caps for the gateposts. Towards the end of the project in September and October, I was then up on a low scaffolding each day, trying to get it finished before my new baby was born. I used to get quite a crowd of sightseers each day watching this crazy pregnant woman, laying bricks and heaving up the stone caps. I found 2 old stone balls to go on top of the stone caps. Finally it was all done and looked great.

Earlier that autumn we had had our good friend Thais Carter from Cambridge Massachusetts to stay with us. She was very sweet with Sarah, and we had some lovely trips out into the country with her. We visited Knole in Sevenoaks, where Rita Sackville West lived, as a child, the autumn sun and colours of the trees in the park were wonderful.

I was surprised to read she was born and always lived in Knole, but when her parents died, as there was no male heir, the house was given to her male cousin! Another crazy law I thought.

Howard Reeve, our doctor, told me in early November that my babies head was engaged and I was ready, so on the next Friday night, November the eighth, I took a bottle of castor oil, and then about 7am the next day I went into labour. Geoff went off to find the midwife who arrived on her bicycle with a basket on the front, with all her gear. She was a very good no fuss and nonsense midwife, and she really suited my temperament very well. When she arrived she had lots of projects that I had to do, help her make up the bed and get everything organised, and then go and make us all a pot of tea! She had an idea that if I sat around, my contractions would not be as strong, so by the time I was allowed into bed I was already at the beginning of my second stage, so it all went very quickly. I had really wanted to have the baby on the weekend, I wanted Geoff to be at home, and Mummy and Daddy would have time to drive down from the north of England, on the Sunday, as they wanted to come down to help me, and Geoff would be free to go back to work on the Monday morning.

Mid-morning on Saturday, the 9th of November I had a baby boy Nils Christopher. I have often thought whether all my building projects during my pregnancy, had got into his blood, as he is now a very busy and excellent builder and architect too!

Unfortunately as it was the damp and foggy November days, Ennie our 'au pair' had caught a flu bug, and so we told her to stay in her room, so when Mummy came down from the North, Ennie was not a lot of help for the first few days. I had painted the large salon—ballroom all white and made some very cheery red curtains over the huge windows. We moved some of our living room furniture in there so I could have friends sitting in there with me and I had the cradle and my bed next to the fireplace. I remember the day Mummy and Daddy arrived and came in to see me, little Sarah went over with her small chair and sat near a large window looking out into the garden. It is very hard for a parent to see the first little one, not be the centre of things anymore, I really felt for her.

Nils' first Christmas we went up to my parents in Sheffield, but Nils had caught a really bad cold from Sarah and her pals, and was on antibiotics. When we got to my parents house we decided to keep Nils in the bathroom at our end of the house, because the central heating made the air very dry, and so the moisture in the bathroom seemed to suit Nils much better, and it always stayed the same temperature. It seemed a sad thing to have to do but I think it was the best place for him. My brother David and his wife Pauline had their first little girl Mandy about the same time that Nils was born, and they were just living on Millhouses Lane, very near to the house on High Wray Close that we had built for my parents.

David by then was in Henry Whitham, Steelworks, Daddy was still there too. Originally David would have liked to study medicine, but as he was the only boy, Daddy thought it would be very sad to see the Steelworks sold after four generations. While we were in

America, David had studied metallurgy at the university and had met his wife Pauline there.

My sister Elizabeth was about twelve years old when Nils was born, she was still at home so we had all different ages of children around. Over the next few years our Christmas crowd got bigger and bigger as our families grew. We always took our au pair girl up with us too, and I think they all enjoyed seeing an English celebration of Christmas.

We had our lower floor all completed about the time Nils was born, so we rented it to two very nice Americans who were over in London acting in the theatre, they had a dog and while they were there, had a little boy who was about Nils' age, called Joshua. Nils and Joshua used to play in our sand pit, which was in the end of the garden and got all the afternoon sun. They got very brown and healthy looking.

We had a little inflatable pool in the garden, and Kent and Maxine, Felix and Anthea's children from the floor above us, and Sarah and Nils and Joshua would all splash in that. I think it was a very hot summer. Sarah and Maxine played together a lot, and the vicar Mr Wedmore who lived opposite had children the same age, who were always across in our big garden.

It was a lovely area to be living in. We went lots of walks over the Heath to Blackheath village, then over to Greenwich Park to see the deer and feed the ducks, and to watch the cricket in summer. If we walked to the end of the road in the park to the statue of James Woolf, (who had stormed the heights of Quebec in Canada,) we got the most amazing views of the Thames curving around back and forth and the whole area of London with the dome of St Paul's very prominent. Our top floor flat had even more of a panoramic view of the whole of London.

On Sundays the heath on Blackheath had dozens of soccer games being played, some of those were very good to watch. Two or three times a year we had a Circus or a Fair come to the side of the heath near to Greenwich Park. Geoff used to walk over with the children to watch them put up the huge Circus tent the night they arrived, it was a very exciting thing to see all the caravans arriving on the heath. The Fair usually came on Bank Holidays, with all sorts of rides—the helter skelter was a big favourite. Every Sunday there were little ponies to ride as well. On Sunday mornings we would often walk over the Heath and down through the park to one of the river pubs, the Cutty Sark or the Yacht, or we would drive into Rotherhithe to the Mayflower pub. (Where the original Mayflower had been built, and was sailed from there, to America.) The children also loved to sail back and forth on the Woolwich ferry, which in those days was a free ride, and it was exciting to see all the cars loaded on and drive off on the other side.

It was a very picturesque place and our children loved to go down to the river and see all the large ocean going ships, cutting across into the big dock area, opposite Greenwich on the Isle of Dogs. There were many shipyards in those days and the docks would be filled with ships from all around the world, they sailed up the Thames as far as Greenwich. The Observatory buildings all opened up as museums, and had amazing astrolabes and old Time Pieces. The Astronomer Royal's house was also opened as a museum and was beautiful inside, lovely panelled rooms, very much like Spencer House, as it was built about the same time, perhaps by the same builders. I remember the Astronomer Royals wonderful padded outfits on display, they were the ones he wore when he had to spend all the night under the opening in his observation dome. The dome has a slot, which opens up, and the astronomer Royal had a special tilted seat so he could observe the night skies through a very large telescope. All of this dated back to 1670 and was very advanced technically. The Greenwich meridian line is a big copper strip running through the Observatory. The time throughout the world is based on the distance from the Greenwich zero meridian line. The children used to stand astride it and enjoy having one foot in the eastern hemisphere and the other in the west.

The museums attached to the Queen's House, (which was designed by Inigo Jones,) down in Greenwich, were all open to the public. They had beautiful naval memorabilia on display, from a Bronze Age ferry boat to an astrolabe from the Armada. The Museum is in the process of a huge remodel and additional gallery space, so it will be well worth a visit in the future.

It was from Greenwich that Admiral Lord Nelson had sailed to the battle of Trafalgar, and where they had returned with his body after the battle, to lie in State. Nils, from being a toddler loved all the paintings of the battles at sea, and the old swords, pistols and uniforms, and many of the exhibits. Perhaps it was from the romance of these stories that he got his longing to go to sea, which he did, when he was older.

One year they put on a 'Son et Lumiere" in Greenwich Park. You sat on the grassy slope and looked towards the river, just below the statue of General James Wolfe (he lived in Macartney House between campaigns after 1751. Eight years later he said his goodbye to this house when he sailed for Quebec and his death. His embalmed body was brought back and lay in state in Macartney House) I wish I had made notes of all the historic events they mentioned in the Son et Lumiere that had taken place there, it was really fascinating. Queen Elizabeth 1st had been born there in the Palace and some little shoes and gardening gloves of hers are on display in a tiny museum in Trinity Hospital Almshouses along with 2 rats that had been found in the old Palace that had brought the plague to London, off one of the boats. The almshouses were built on the river east of the Palace in 1613, and were for retired old sailors. I helped organise two Garden Parties there for the Greenwich Society, and there were still some old sailors living there. It is still there and is a charming little building. There had also been a whale washed up in Greenwich, which everyone took to be a bad omen!

I have always loved history and visualising the costumes and people of those times. I remember in Pepys' Diaries at the time of the Fire of London, he and a group of friends had all driven out in their carriages to the same hill in Greenwich, and had watched the great fire consume London from there. As we had such a historical house it made all the past come very alive for me. I had several books of costumes of that period when Spencer House was built, and I have a list of the occupants of the house, many of them connected with the Royal Palace in Greenwich, so I could imagine the scenes that must have taken place in the grand entrance hall and in the ballroom. Felix Barker our friend who lived on the first floor above us, did wonderful research in the British Museum, he came up with a list of the occupants and all their dates.

The occupants of Spencer House.

It had previously been converted into a military training college, later a riding school, and in the late 1880's it became a girls boarding school.

1680 George Legge (later Baron Dartmouth) completed the house. His son became Viscount Lewisham and Earl of Dartmouth.

1689 to 1700 Sir Martin Beckman, the Earl of Dartmouth was moved to the Tower of London.

1700 to 1728 Richard Symes, the tenth son of Thomas Symes. His widow stayed in the house until approximately 1750.

1753 Richard Hall, a naval officer.

1762 Lucius Cary the 7th Viscount Falkland.

1785 Sarah his widow acquired the house. She was also the widow of the Earl of Suffolk.

1797 to 1804 Alexander Trotter, a Scotsman, landed proprietor, he came perhaps because of the golf.

1808 to 1810 the Honourable William Wellesley Polehr, became the third Earl of Hornington, the brother of the Duke of Wellington.

1810 to 1812 Thomas, the fifth Earl of Selkirk. His son and heir, was born in the house.

1814 to 1822 John Viscount Perceval takes the house, the grandson of the 2nd Earl of Egmont, and half nephew of Spencer Perceval. Spencer Perceval's father, the second Earl of Egmont, lived at Charlton House, as tenants of Jane Wilson family.

1824 to 1828 Sir Charles Bagot. His brother the 2nd Earl Bagot, had married one of the Earl of Dartmouth's daughters.

1828 Captain Gregg

1835 to 1850 Miss Sapienta Stone, ran a ladies boarding school.

1850 Charlotte and Elena Mary Bohun took over the school. They had a previous school at 3 Eliot Place.

1858 Reverend Theophilus Menziels.

1860 to 1885. William Keizer, military training college. (Captain of Blackheath Golf Club)

1890 divided into two houses, Spencer House and Perceval House.

1890 to 1925, Misses Young. Their photographs taken in the house are now in the Blackheath Society and show the interior of our house with gas mantles on the walls, and I think they had changed the windows, doing away with the small panes.

1927 to 1930 the house was empty then sold by the Earl of Dartmouth in 1930. Divided into flats. (The Dartmouth Family had owned it since 1670 but they lived in Dartmouth House, next door to us and all the various occupants had been their tenants.

1956 June Holroyd and Geoffrey Holroyd bought the house.

A drawing of the house in 1830 is in the British Museum in London.

Here is a brief history of the area, from Felix Barker's research. I hope you enjoy History as much as I do. Here goes with Felix's information.

Traces of ancient settlements have been found. The Romans built Watling Street across Blackheath wastes (probably on the line now taken by Shooters Hill and the Old Dover Road) and built houses nearby. Blackheath was an essential section of the London to Rochester Roman defence lines. Traces of the Roman occupation can still be seen in Greenwich Park and Roman remains were found in Dartmouth Row during the digging in the Kitchen Garden of Dartmouth House, which was once the home of the Earl of Dartmouth. (Dartmouth House is the house next to Spencer House)

Ancient Barrows, or tumuli, probably of fifth or sixth century origin have been found on the slopes of the Heath, near Crooms Hill, and these were excavated during the late eighteenth-century. To continue this brief history it is necessary to explain out of context, that Blackheath was once extensively quarried for deposits of chalk, limestone, sand, and gravel. The soil here is pebbly and loose and geologically the area is known as the Blackheath tertiary beds. Beneath the pebble beds are layers of clay and sand and beneath these a thick layer of chalk. At the escarpment of the Point the chalk is nearer to the surface than at any other place.

In 1780 a large cavern, cut in solid rock, was discovered consisting of several large areas connected by passages, the whole reaching a depth of a hundred and sixty feet. At the bottom of the cavern the floor of which was fine dry sand, was a 27 ft deep well. Some authorities think this may have been the "chalkpytte" mentioned in a 15th century lease. But there is a strong theory that the local people, frightened by the invading Danes, dug the original cavities as Dene holes, or hiding holes, and that these had been extended subsequently.

During the 1850's the public were admitted to the caverns. In 1853 a 'Bal Masque' was held there, but a wag (joker) or lack of oxygen, doused the candle lights and panic ensued. As a result the entrance in Blackheath Hill, was filled in and the caves remained sealed—but the legends grew wildly. (A note added in February 2003—I have just been told by friends still living in the area, that Blackheath Hill, which is the hill coming up to the end of Dartmouth Row onto Blackheath, has just collapsed down into the old chalk pits. Luckily some pedestrians in the area were able to stop cars on the bottom of the hill, before they fell into a deep cave. Traffic was diverted off the hill for approximately a year) *Tales of secret passages from Blackheath to the Queen's House in Greenwich Park, and even a still strongly held belief that they connect, eventually with Chislehurst caves. I think this must sadly be discounted.*

In 1938 the caverns were once more opened with a view to assessing the suitability for air raid shelters. The entrance had been forgotten and a fresh shaft was sunk in Maidenstone Hill. Traces of the notorious masked Ball were found and a number of souvenirs taken for the local museums, but it was felt that the caves would not be ample proof against Hitler's Blitzkrieg, and the entrance was sealed for the second time.

Various conduits have been found under the Heath and a substantial brick tunnel stretches across The Grove and down Hyde Vale. This and other conduits supplied water to the Palace and Hospital in Greenwich.

When I was digging deeply to plant a tree at the back of Spencer House, I dug into one of these tunnels. I hit some brick vaults and was able to lift out one or two bricks from the arched roof, and look down with a flashlight into a very substantial tunnel. I quickly replaced it all as I thought if I announced it, I would have all the local historic and archeological buffs digging up my whole garden, which I was just planting, to find where the tunnel lead. It was perhaps a water conduit, but at the time I thought it might have been an escape tunnel so that it would be possible to get from Spencer House down to the Palace, as we have heard those did exist. Blackheath had had several violent periods, with battles on the heath, various rebellions, and because it was the main Dover Road it had had a history of highwaymen, waiting to rob the wealthy travelers crossing the heath, which was very bare and treeless, and anyone leaving London to cross the Channel to France had to travel that road.

My other discovery when I was planting a tree near the swimming pool, was a beautiful gold sovereign, of young Queen Victoria, minted in 1860. It is like a perfect newly minted coin. Mummy wanted me to dig up the whole area as she said people in those days often buried their savings, as there were no banks, and she thought there would be more than one. I still have the coin in my safety deposit box.

Spencer House projects begin

I think the first really big project I tackled was to replace the cornice missing from the front of the house, which had been destroyed by a bomb that landed next to the house in the 2nd World War. The cornice had housed a big box gutter, lined with lead, which all had to be replaced. This was very important as the rain ran from the roof and ran down the wall where there was no gutter. We needed scaffolding across the front of the house, and all the dentils (carved corbels at the roof line) had to be carefully matched with the existing.

The roof was a 'Mansard' roof,—a steep part first behind the box gutter, that was covered in slate, with dormer windows, but then the whole of the middle of the roof was flat and was roofed in lead, rolled lead, the same as St. Pauls Cathedral. While the box gutter was done they made repairs to the lead roof. This was a continuing problem, as the lead was the original from 1670 and it moved a little in the hot sun, creating cracks, which would leak in the next rains.

The long and short stonework, down all the corners of the house, as well as the stone stringcourses and the stone keystones, had all been painted, probably since the house was first built. I sent some chips of paint away to be analyzed and found there were 67 different layers of paint, so any chipped paint left a very deep hole, so I decided as I was not pregnant, to climb up long ladders and burn off the layers of paint back to the original stone. The keystones are like the Dartmouth's Westminster property in Queen Anne's Gate, lively faces with distinguishing features, they really looked like portraits of actual people, over each window. Unfortunately with their thick layers of paint many of their features were lost, so I decided to burn off the paint on those and get them back to the original stone. I remember as I held my blow torch on their faces, paint poured out of their nostrils and ears and any deep facial crevices, it was a very exciting project and I couldn't tell what effect it would all be until I had it finished and then it looked great and I decided worth my while.

The brickwork joints had been very poorly patched over the years. Of course the pointing was the original from 1670. A lot of it was very soft and was absorbing rain, so I decided to have it re-pointed. The brick walls were very thick so we had no problem with damp coming through, but in the cold weather once the moisture got through the pointing and into the face of the bricks, the frost cracked off the face of the bricks, so it would have gradually destroyed all the brick face. The pointing in the original house had all been tuck-pointing and I had a difficult time to find anyone still doing that. Finally I was able to find an old firm that was still doing tuck-pointing. They first took out the soft mortar joints and troweled them flush with new cement mortar. When it was all dried out, a thin white line was ruled in the centre of the cement joint, giving it a very elegant appearance. A few of the bricks were missing or broken so those were replaced. This had one of the biggest effects of any of my projects.

I re-painted the windows of the first two floors of the house, but got some painting firm to do the top two floors and cornices, which were all in timber. Fixing up such a beautiful house was such an exciting project. Each time I had saved up enough of the rents coming in, I was able to make another huge improvement, and extend the life of the house for maybe another three hundred years. All my projects were slowly achieved, over a period of nine or ten years work. I think that continual maintenance is essential with any building, but especially the very old ones.

Another important thing I did for our flat was to put in oil-fired boilers and central heating, as the very large rooms were very hard to heat. Geoffrey did not want to have any pipes showing from the heating, because of the beautiful paneling, so the heating firm we were using agreed to take all the pipes under the floors. As soon as we pulled up some of the floorboards we found the spaces between joists were completely full of 300 years of dust and debris. Someone also had a theory that a lot of the dust and sawdust debris might have been their way of providing sound insulation from floor to floor.

The heating engineers had not allowed for all that cleaning in the estimate, so I said I would do that. I removed board by board and got everything cleaned out. Many of the joists had been pegged for ships timbers, and must have been brought up from the naval shipyards in Greenwich. Over the years the joists had had a large amount of timber destroyed by deathwatch beetle. I was worried whether the strength of the floor joists was still sufficient. I got a chisel and hacked them back to the strong wood, some of the joists were so bad that they had quite a dip, so we got a builder in to add a new joist on either side of the old original one, so the support for boards was pretty straight. It was a huge job I ended up with a mountain of debris from under the floors and it was piled in the front garden about 10 ft high by 15 ft wide. Among the debris I found some interesting things, a lot of oyster shells, and broken clay pipes. They had been very long ones, and I imagine after Big Banquets these objects were swept into a loose floorboard. I found one or two snake skeletons. They must have found some way of getting in there. I also found a number of marbles, from a very old game, as they were made of marble. Nowadays marbles, for the game are all made of glass.

When I was working on a room in the front of the house I was surprised to see through the floorboards a room that had no ceiling to it, so I could look straight down into this old room which was completely sealed off with no doors and without any access to it any more. It had a very old fireplace and looked like it had never been used for many years, part of a very odd remodel at some time.

We had more vaulted wine cellars on the lower floor, so I had a large metal oil tank welded in one vaulted storeroom, in another the hot water system, and another for the furnace for heating. What a difference that made to our enjoyment of the big rooms.

The one huge problem we discovered, which had no solution, was that the other half of the house, Perceval House, was owned by the most ridiculous man called Nightingale. He had written his own blurb in 'Who's Who' (apparently everyone does write their own, so they can lie about themselves, they always seem to be too good to be true) and called himself 'a preserver of old buildings.' He preserved nothing. His family lived in the basement of their half of the house, that was so damp, when it rained his wife wore rubber Wellington boots as it was standing in water. He had leaks continually coming in, in the big entrance hall, from gutters and broken cast iron rain water pipes, which produced huge growths of dry rot, these got through into our half of the house.

Unfortunately when the house was divided into two, in the late 19th century, the same timbers in the floor joists and in the roof still continued through the party wall, and brought his dry rot through to us. I had members of the National Historic Buildings Trust down to see our problem, which was continuous, and they wrote to Nightingale, but it did no good at all. He owned another house in Blackheath, which suffered the same way. It had had a beautiful pedimented wooden porch over the front door, which he allowed to rot so badly it had to be taken off. He destroyed all the beautiful old buildings he bought, he seemed to be interested only in getting the rent money into his own pockets and none of it was put into any maintenance. He had been hoping to buy our portion of the house, but luckily for the house we bought it, it was really essential to have a person who knew how much maintenance had to be put in, to such priceless old monuments.

I don't know if you have experienced dry rot, it is a fungus growth that devours wood and spreads very rapidly if there is any damp, which there always is in England. The wood is destroyed and loses all its strength and is crumbly like mould. Whenever it rained heavily

I would go outside with an umbrella and check that my down pipes and gutters were all working well, the box gutters needed to be free of any leaves etc and I had the cast iron down pipes replaced as the old ones were brittle and cracked very easily. We were continually having small outbreaks of dry rot which I got treated straight way.

Ennie, who was our current au pair girl from Helsinki, was enjoying her stay in London so much, that she asked us if she could spend another year with us. She wanted to visit Finland for the summer to see her grandmother and friends. I really needed someone living in to help, as I was very busy all the time on projects on the house. We were very lucky as we found a great Italian girl Paola Bresciani, who just wanted to come to London for the summer. She was from Bologna, and I think, rather a wealthy family.

Nils was by then seven or eight months old and was a very sweet little guy, Paola could not stop kissing him, she said his mouth was so kissable, how could we not kiss him all the time! She was very vivacious and when she got ready to go off to town she looked great, wonderful tailored clothes and she piled her hair up on her head, but when she was working in the house she would be in an old cotton house dress with her hair down and no make-up, she was hard to recognise as the same person. In her short stay in London she had so many boy friends coming down to find her, popping their heads in the windows to see if it was her room!

Some of our friends thought it would be too worrying having a teenager au pair to deal with every year, but I didn't feel I needed to keep my eye on them when they were not in our house, in their free time. If their parents had allowed them to come to London, which everyone knew was a very swinging City, then it was not my job to have them answer to me for all their free time. Sometimes they came home terribly late, but the public transport was very difficult to find after 11pm. and as long as they were there to help me get the children up, and breakfast done, then I didn't worry. None of them got pregnant, or had any problems whilst they were with us, and they all loved the London scene, which began to be really swinging at the end of the 50's and early 60's.

In 1956 Geoff was part of the Independent Group who put on an exhibition at the Whitechapel Art Gallery, 'This Is Tomorrow'. Some great people were part of the group, Peter and Alison Smithson, James Stirling, Reyner Banham, Eduardo Paolozzi, and William Turnbull. It received great acclaim and has just recently been redone, opening at the Institute of Contemporary Art in London, then traveled to Spain, and then to MOCA in Los Angeles, and then up to Berkeley, California. Geoff still had his display panels (I had lugged them around for him all those years, through the move to the states so he was able to use the originals.) In 1958 Geoff started teaching at the Architecture Association, which was an excellent school for students in those days. Peter and Alison Smithson were teaching there, and Ron Heron from Archigram, it was a very lively scene.

His main project was all the design work on the Sanderson Building, a very large design project, six story building, four blocks with an inner court designed as a show room for Sanderson products, Fabrics for curtains, wallpapers and floor coverings. The building was finished and opened in 1960. It was very well received by Ivan Sanderson and had a lot of publicity in Architectural Press. Vogue magazine did a big photo shoot with all their models there, and also in the very elegant Courtyard. He was very pleased with it's success.

When Nils was one year old, I became pregnant again and on August the 15th 1959, I had a dear little girl. I had my old midwife Mrs. Rowe and had my bed in the same large room where Nils was born, and Howard Reeve was again my doctor. Sarah was very delighted with the new baby and loved to help me bath her.

We always had a very hard time to think of the new baby's name—we waited until after they were born, and Geoff would bring home the American dictionary of names and all sorts of books. We were really stuck for a new name, but you do have six weeks to decide on one in England, and during that time we went up to the theatre one night, to see a Russian play and there was a girl called Tatiana, that everyone called Tanya, and Tanya Elg was famous then as a ballet dancer. We never thought of a second name, so Tanya has always been rather disappointed that she only has the one name. At that time we didn't know anyone called Tanya so it was quite original.

Because she was born on August 15th, Geoff and I didn't really get a holiday so we decided in February 1960 to go off to Serfaus in Austria, skiing. We took Nils who was two, and Sarah who was four, with us, but we left Tanya with our good friends Tom and Pam Margerison (Tom had been my flat-mate in Chester Square just before I got married) who lived in Dulwich and they had two boys of their own, they all four loved our baby girl, and she knew them well.

Sarah and Nils used to get terribly excited anticipating something like that trip, so I put them to bed at the usual time and didn't tell them that we were going. About 11pm when we were all packed and ready to leave I woke them up and got them dressed and we went off to the airport. It was a wonderful break as Geoff and I had both been so busy. The small hotel where we stayed was very informal. Serfaus was a pretty, farming and country village, one where the cows spent all the winter on the ground floor of the houses, and the people lived up above. We took it in turns to ski half the day each, and the other one went for walks or sledging with the children. We went over to St Moritz for the day, and found the whole area was really beautiful in the snow. It was such a lovely change from London in the winter, which always had leaden skies and damp and often raining.

My parents had bought a small country house in South Creake, Norfolk. Daddy's youngest sister, Joan, had married a man from Fakenham in Norfolk. He was in the Barclays Bank there. We used to go up to South Creake a lot in the summer, and many winter weekends, as it was such a lovely wild area for the children to run free. They all kept wellington boots, rain gear, fishing rods and nets in the store there. That part of England is very unspoiled; it used to be the wealthiest area of England in the 16th century, and has an amazing history going back to 400,000 BC when tools were made from local flints. Around 125,000 BC the area was covered by Wolstonian ice sheet. By 8000 BC the climate was getting milder and new groups of people were moving from the Continent to eastern England. In 7,000-6,000 BC the rising sea level finally cut the land link between Britain and Europe. Settlements from 6,500 and 3,500 BC have been found. The most important source of flints in Norfolk was Grimes Graves near Thetford. We used to drive on the road past Grimes Graves, and climbed down the shafts to the flint faces many times. Geoff and I were just there recently, it is now very organized, and quite touristy.

The tribes of southern Britain were constantly at war with each other in the years before the Roman invasion. When the Romans landed on the south coast in AD 43 the kingdoms south of the Thames were quickly defeated. The Iceni in Norfolk had probably formed an alliance with Rome and managed to remain an independent kingdom. Roman goods began to appear in Norfolk, and Roman coins replaced local ones. This peaceful position of the Iceni ended violently in AD 60. King Prasutagas thought he had an agreement with Nero that upon his death, he would take only half of Prasutigas' lands, dividing the rest between his two daughters.

When the King died, the Roman army took advantage and overran the whole area. The King's widow, Boudicca (Queen Boadicea) with her own army, led a revolt, which was joined by the Trinovantes. The Iceni rebels captured the Romanised town of Camulodunum (Colchester) and laid it waste, and also destroyed Verulamium (St. Albans) and Londinium (London). The majority of the Roman forces had been in Anglesey, off the coast of North Wales, but they returned and met the rebels north of London and defeated them. Boudicca died, probably by her own hand.

I really love this story. There is a statue of her on the Thames embankment riding in her chariot with knives or swords sticking out from her chariot wheels, to cut through the Roman soldiers! She seems like a wonderful tough Amazonian woman, and I know the Iceni were very big, tall people. She must have been a terrifying enemy to meet.

In more recent times, Norfolk was very prosperous in the wool trade, in the 16th Century, and because of the wealth it had some wonderful churches, country houses etc. There were so many churches with beautiful brasses, commemorating members of the wealthy families upon their deaths. We decorated the walls of Mummy and Daddy's cottage in South Creake with some beautiful brass rubbings. Geoff and I rubbed the big brass in Felbrigg, which is one of the very famous ones. We hung it down the stair well in the cottage in South Creake. As the children got older they used to love to rub the smaller brasses too, and Nils enjoyed rubbing the knights in armour. They had the most elaborate hinged elbow and knee joint details, to allow them to move. The big Felbrigg brass has two figures on it, Sir Simon Fellbrigg in armour with his feet on a lion (denoting he died in battle) and next to him is a very young girl, in the most elaborate beautiful dress, she was the niece of Good King Wenceslas, (famous from the carol we sing at Christmas) and she came over to England to marry Sir Simon when she was only a young girl. Just after they were married he went off to the Crusades and she, poor girl died while he was away, probably from being stranded in a strange country, miles from anywhere, no one speaking her language and strange English food. She is buried under the brass in the Felbrigg Church. When he returned from the Crusades he married again and is buried in Norwich Cathedral.

The Felbrigg brass is huge, 8ft high by 4ft 6ins wide and it was impossible to find a paper that wide, but when Sarah and Tanya were older I was able to find a roll of special 'Felbrigg' paper made for this brass, so the 2 girls rubbed it with heel ball (it is the black wax material that shoemakers used to blacken the ends of the layers of leather that built up the heel of a shoe.) We still have the big brass rubbing, I had it mounted. It shows very clearly in the photo later, taken in a house we built in Las Alturas.

Admiral Horatio Nelson was born in 1758 in a small village Burnham Thorpe just near South Creake, in Norfolk, and the little

Church where his father was the vicar, has some wonderful brasses too. Amazing to be brought up in such a primitive country spot and to be made Admiral of the fleet and move to such high society circles. When I saw Laurence Olivier as Nelson and Vivien Leigh in the film I could clearly think of what his life had been originally, and what his wife from such a small village would have been like, and how much he had been able to achieve for himself.

There are a lot of castles in that area that the children loved to explore. We used to take picnics out for the day, and go to beautiful sandy beaches, old windmills, and quaint little villages, it was a very good area to explore. Opposite the house was the Creek, and it had water flowing in it in those days, so the children in their wellington boots and with fishing nets caught jars of little minnows. The cottage next to ours had a family from Birmingham with two children the same ages as our older two, so we did lots of outings with them.

After a few years they decided to sell their house, so we told some of our good friends in Blackheath, Lois and Peter Day, who had returned to London from San Francisco, and they bought the house. They still go there a lot and their children use it too. They had a daughter Sarah who was about the same age as our Sarah, Timon their son was a little older, and a daughter Sophie was Nils' age. Later they had one more girl Cressida who was the same age as my youngest, Sam. They were a perfect gang together. Lois and Peter had a sailboat, which they kept up in Brancaster Staithe.

When Geoff and I returned from the States we got our flat in Great James Street from Paul and Sylvia Poulson, you may remember. They had moved out because she was expecting a baby, but poor Sylvia had a miscarriage. She had finally had a girl, Suzanne who was the same age as Nils. Paul had gone off with someone else, so Sylvia and her mother bought a little new house in Brancaster, Norfolk. Sylvia had been a fabric designer for Horrockses in London, but in Norfolk she was teaching at Hunstanton school, the very modern 'brutalist' school that our friends Peter and Alison Smithson had designed, after winning a competition, when we were all first in London. Anyway we always saw Sylvia and Suzanne when we were up, and of course saw my Aunt Joan frequently in Fakenham, she enjoyed our children a lot as she never had any children, but she and Douglas had a lot of little pug dogs and one Corgie.

We used to go up for 2 or 3 weeks vacation in the summer to Norfolk. Geoffrey came up by train on the weekends but I stayed up there with the au pair girl and the children. For two or three summers we rented a house in Dartmouth in Devon for a change. That is a beautiful part of England too, and Geoffrey came down by train on Friday evenings to join us for the weekends there, and we went across on the ferry to the station on the other side of the estuary of the river Dart, to meet him. The first two summers we were very lucky with the weather, but the last year when we had my sister Elizabeth with us too, it rained every single day. I had a hard time to keep everyone busy, we went to every museum within miles, and all the cinemas I could find!

Elizabeth always visited us regularly as she enjoyed the children and she was like an older sister to them. She was ten years older than Sarah. After her Hunmanby (where I went to) schooling was over she came down to London to study music at the Academy and used to enjoy coming to stay on the weekends with us at Spencer House. She met a boy Howard Rooke from Manchester at the Academy, and they both came down to stay with us too. They got married and after they got their degrees in London, they got teaching jobs near Bournemouth so we didn't see them so often.

Elizabeth had a baby boy Michael while they were down south. Later they got teaching jobs in Norfolk and for a while lived in Reepham, they had another baby boy Martin, and a little girl, Thomasin, now they have a lovely house in Blakeney, looking over the harbour and out to sea. They are both teaching at Gresham's school in Holt and during term time they live there, as Elizabeth is housemother to the young girls and Howard teaches music.

Elizabeth still teaches some piano lessons and together they put on wonderful concerts, choral and orchestral. Howard has done very well as a conductor and Elizabeth plays the organ and piano. Recently Howard and Elisabeth retired from the school, sold their house in Blakeney, and moved to Little Dartmouth in Devon. Even more recently, in 2008, they have moved back to Norfolk. I think they felt a long way off from their two children. Michael still lives in Norfolk, and Thomasin in London, the other son Martin lives in Grenoble, in France.

Geoffrey and I took our holidays together later, without the children, after all the schools had gone back. Geoff never enjoyed days on the beach with the children. When they were small I took them with the au pair girl up to my parents, who enjoyed them visiting on their own.

Geoffrey and I flew to Athens one summer and visited Professor and Effie Michelis, who we had got to know so well in Harvard in 1952. It was lovely to see them again. We spent a lot of time walking around the old Greek remains on the Parthenon, and made several trips around outside of Athens. We then went up to Thesalonika the same year and explored all the architecture there. The Greeks showed us many buildings and statues that the Turks had smashed up on their way through, and then when we were in Turkey later on, we heard all the terrible stories of the Greeks and the destruction they had caused!

Another summer we went to Yugoslavia, we flew to Zagreb, and then went down the coast by boat, staying in Split, Hvar, Rab and Dubrovnik. The Palace of Diocletian in Split (Spoleto) was amazing, a vast place with all sorts of families living in different parts of it. We sailed down the coast, and spent the longest time in Dubrovnik, which was a beautiful walled City. It was a strange time to be there, Tito was in power and it was a very Communist country. We stayed in a beautiful old hotel in Dubrovnik, very elegant old buildings. The manager was the top guy in the local Communist organization, and wore funny short sleeve 'T' shirts and looked very out of place in such an elegant building. I think he had never learned how to run a large hotel. A friend of ours, an architect was arrested when he went there, for taking a photo of a school!

Whilst we were in Dubrovnik I used to go to the beach near our hotel quite often to swim, and I met a boy called Jakov. He was very interested to use his English, and asked Geoffrey and me to visit his family in the town. We went there several times as we always found it was very informative to meet and visit local people in a new country we didn't know. They had a tall stone house with all kinds of family members living in it. In the toilet, I remember, was a large rock on the floor and we were asking Jakov why it was there, and he said the toilet was a huge shaft drilled through the rock and when the sea got stormy the water would splash up so they had to put the rock on it to seal it!

Each morning Jakov's old grandfather would be up and out really early, and I asked Jakov if he still had to work at his age, but he said no, he was dashing off to the beach to see all the girl tourists in bikinis. The local women were always covered up in black outfits and so this sight of so many bodies, he couldn't resist!

They were a muslim family, 'musslimen' as Jakov called them. I read the history of Yugoslavia whilst I was there, it had been taken over by so many countries Austria, Italy, Turkey and several others, and was a real mixture of people. Recently they have been carrying out their 'ethnic cleansing,' which in Yugoslavia has meant the massacre of one group by another. It had remnants of all their buildings. The town of Dubrovnic was very fascinating. It had a wide main street the 'Ploce' which people said had originally been water, but had been filled in. Every evening the whole town was out in their best clothes, walking up and down and checking everybody out. You could also walk around a walkway on top of the walls, that circled the city, they were still all intact.

The harbour was a very ideal half moon shape and this had a chain across the mouth, which could be raised in case of any troubles, to keep out enemy vessels.

Jakov said how they had all been very content with their simple life, until all the tourists had started going there, with their cameras and gear that we all had, plus I imagine the American films, which were shown all over in Greece and Italy and Yugoslavia, had made them envious and unsettled. Before we left Jakov asked for our London address, in case he was ever over there.

Two or three weeks after we got home the doorbell rang quite late on a Sunday night, and there was Jakov with a huge suitcase! Luckily I had our lower floor flat in Spencer House empty at that time, so he stayed down there. He was supposed to be over in London to find a job, but he never really got off to town to start to look. He borrowed our record player and lounged about with records on all the time. We had a very brisk Dutch au pair, Marianne, and when she was going to town one afternoon I asked her to take Jakov. He started out with her from our house, she was a tall girl and really stepped out, and Jakov with hands in his pockets, ambled along behind her. He had apparently lost her before they got to Lewisham station, just down the hill from us, so he just ambled back again.

Sarah was just three and was quite afraid of him as he had very black curly hair and black curly beard and was always washing his hair and would come up with towels all around his head. He gave up the idea of a job hunt after a week or two and went back home. We got letters from him periodically. One-day he was back ringing our doorbell again, this time he was in a uniform. He was a guide bringing Yugoslavs to tour around London! Wonder where they all are now?

We stayed in a beautiful old Venetian Palace in Hvar, that they had made into a hotel, but it was very dirty, looked great though. Hvar was a wonderful town, it had the earliest Venetian theatre, the oldest one ever. When I got back to London I got a weird dysentery type bug that was a notifiable one to the Health Authorities. The Health authorities came and sprayed everything I might have touched, and I had to go every two weeks and have tests to see if I still had it. It took about six months before I was clear. Howard Reeve our Doctor said there was no point in taking antibiotics to clear it, as it would just keep returning. I had to wait until my body built up resistance and cleared itself. Nils was a small baby so I had to be very careful, and continually washing my hands.

Some architect friends of ours, Gordon and Ursula Bowyer went with their children to the same old Palace, after us, and their son got so ill they had to get a helicopter to fly him off to an Italian hospital. It was a pretty rough country in those days.

Another summer our big vacation trip was to Turkey. We flew to Istanbul and almost the very first morning we were walking by the Blue Mosque when a young fellow came and started to talk to us. He thought we were Americans, and he was in the Turkish air force and wanted to go to the States, to continue his flying training. He had an exam paper that he needed help on, so we sat in a café and went through his papers. The questions were very baffling, even to me. I remember one 'If you were in church and a number of planes flew low, drowning out the service, should you (1) be pleased that your air force was working for your defense, or (2) should you criticise them for their noise, or—(3) some other thing. Luckily Geoff had just read a book that he felt had given him the clue for the correct answers.

We sat for about two hours completing his forms, and then he said as he was on leave he would love to show us all around Istanbul. We had some wonderful tours with him, over the Bosphorous to Uskadar, on a Sunday when everyone was out flying beautiful home made paper kites. Santa Sophia, Top Kapi, and down to the old water cisterns (the ones that were in one of the James Bond films) and then he took us on a bus trip, out of the centre to a suburb where his family all lived. It was a small house on a very dusty dirt road that had quite heavy traffic, so all the windows in the 'parlor' were lost in dust. They had arranged dining type chairs all around the walls in the parlor, and we sat and had some very refreshing tea in little glasses. In the back of the house they had a small building where they were making all kinds of plastic things. They had a huge pile of 'mechanics illustrated' and had used those to learn how to work with the newly invented 'plastic'. They gave us several things that they had made. It is always so great to have an actual family to visit, in any country. We saw lots of things we would never have found.

We made a trip down the coast to Izmir, and found a Hotel right on the water. It was a very romantic place, then during the night all the clop clop of a huge herd of goats being driven along the quay, outside our hotel. We wanted to go to see the excavations at Ephesus, so we got a taxi, to take us there. It was early days in that dig and I know by now they have found many more wonderful buildings. I remember the stone street with shops on it and the beginning of the temple.

The area round there was growing lots of cherries, and some of the women with their children looked so photogenic, but we were told they did not like you to take their photos as they felt you took something away from them. On our return to Istanbul before our trip home, our friend came round to our Hotel with some beautiful paper kites he had made for our children. We heard from him later that he did go to the States to do more training, so I guess Geoff's answers must have been O.K.

One Easter holiday, I think it was 1961. I rented a house for all the family in Antibes in the south of France. We decided as it was such a long drive and as I was the only driver it would be the best to put the car on the train when we got across the Channel and travel down on a sleeper to Lyons. Geoff always used the public transport and in England at this time driving was something not everyone practiced. We were all 6 going, Geoff and I, Karna our Danish au pair, Sarah, Nils and Tanya (who was almost two). I explained to Karna that the water on the trains was 'non potable' (not OK to drink) and we would use only bottled water. Anyway she had gone ahead and cleaned her teeth with it, I guess not thinking that it was the same as drinking it, so when we got to Antibes she spent all the time sick in bed, so was not much help with the children.

It was a lovely area to be in, we went along to Monte Carlo and St. Tropez and the children enjoyed our nearest beach Juan les Pins. They had pedallos you could rent on the water, and the beach was beautifully raked each morning with very comfortable lounge chairs, all very luxurious. Our house was just near the Picasso museum, and we really enjoyed the market and the shopping for food. On our drive to and from the train in Lyons we went via Arles and Nimes, and saw the Roman theatre and Pont du Gard, the famous Roman Aquaduct: we have a film of the children doing the twist in the Roman Theatre in Nimes.

The Twist was all the rage at the time, and Karna had a boyfriend called Bipin, and he had so many of the Beatles records that he brought down, 'Twist and Shout' seemed to be the happening event. Bipin's family, were from India, but were living in Zanzibar in Africa. They were spice importers and I think a wealthy family. They had sent Bipin to be educated in England, and the poor boy had been instructed by his father as part of their religion, that he must never eat meat, nor drink alcohol, or smoke. At first he had been in a boarding house where the cook had no idea about cooking vegetables, and after a year of almost starving to death, he had started to live like the English. When Karna got to know him he was eating meat and smoking and drinking too, and was terrified what his father would do, if he ever found out.

Karna's family came over from Denmark and met Bipin and really liked him, they had no Indians in Denmark, and they had no prejudices, and were happy that she was planning to marry him. Poor Bipin though was certain that his father would disown him when he found out he was going to marry Karna. I think they were married but I don't know for sure and I wonder where they would go to live?

(This puzzle has now been solved!! It is August 2003, and I received a phone call from Karna, who is now living in New York! She looked on the internet to do a search for me, and had traced me to Santa Barbara, California.

She had returned to Denmark when she left us, and Bipin had kept in touch with her, and invited her back to London. They were married there, but it was in 1965, when Geoff and I were in the US for Geoff's lecture tour, so we missed the invitation. They were living in several places in Africa, Bipin was working as an accountant. They had 2 boys who are now in their 30's. Bipin was asked by his company to come to the US to work. He is now retired, they have a summer house in the Hamptons, and an apartment in NY City. Isn't it amazing to be able to track down such old lost friendships? We are looking forward to seeing them soon in California.) (another note to add to this, Karna and Bipin have just been here to Santa Barbara to stay with us, in the spring of 2004. They were still a very good pair, Karna was delighted to see all the children again, and Bipin is a really sweet guy—very bright. We took them to the Danish town of Solvang, and to La Purissima Mission, as they didn't know too much about California History.)

We had a lot of parties in those days as we had the lovely big room, which was ideal. Every November we had a huge party for children, which became a real tradition, Nils had a birthday November 9th, and Sarah's was on Nov 24th. It was like an early Christmas Party, they were always Fancy Dress and we all enjoyed them. Every year we had a clown called Smokey who did magic tricks, and played lots of musical instruments and organised games for them to play. All our own friends brought their children, Peter and Alison Smithson with Simon and Samantha, David and Beryl Allford with Jane, Simon and Sally, John and Brenda Maddox with Joey, and then all the local children from the different schools and the neighbourhood, it was always a wonderful occasion. We also had several New Years Eve parties, which we shared with Felix and Anthea, we found we could get a large crowd in our big room. It was of course the original ballroom.

I was having a big party in the winter and cooked continuously for several days. When I cook a large amount of food, I don't like to keep tasting things. I had decided one of the dishes I would make was my American recipe for chili con carne. I searched the shops in Blackheath for chili powder, but no one had it, but they had ground chilies, which I thought must be the same. When Geoff came in from the office in the evening he got a spoon and had a taste, he was in agony! It was <u>SO HOT</u>, He was hopping all around, I added more beans and lots more tomatoes, but I could not get it to cool down, so I bought a big piece of beef to roast instead, and put my chili into two plastic buckets. A couple of nights later our au pair girl was going to a party, and most of the boys were from India, so I asked her if she would like to take my chili with her. It was apparently a tremendous success, everyone was saying "I cannot believe an English woman could cook this" they really loved it! I was so pleased that Geoff had had a taste, imagine the scene with lots of English folk with their very mild tastes, they would have just about passed out!

Geoff was still very busy working on the new showrooms for Sandersons. The working drawings were very complicated as the contractors in England had never built that type of building, it was one of the first there. He was doing all the drawings himself too and arranging details such as having John Piper to do a large stained glass wall behind the main staircase. In the courtyard in the centre he got very specially designed with large trees and a huge granite slab brought in from Wales. The building was completed in 1960. Sandersons were terribly pleased with their new showrooms. Currently in 1998 Geoff has some very exciting news about Sandersons, but I will get to that later.

A letter I sent to my parents after a spectacular party, around this time.

Spencer House, Wednesday.

I must just write to you straight away and tell you about the fabulous party we went to last night. Today it seems like a dream, as I never knew such parties could exist! We went to the Mike Todd party to Premiere his "Round the World in 80 days" He had taken over Battersea Gardens for the party, (the ones Geoff had designed for the Festival of Britain, in 1951.)

We all went by boat from Westminster about midnight, all the boats left together and looked so beautiful with bands playing on the deck, and several bars on each boat. We were all given raincoats to keep, about 2000 of us, but luckily it didn't rain and was a beautiful warm night. The people there were so fabulous, Todd himself and his wife Elizabeth Taylor, who is pregnant, but had a wonderful designer dress and looked great. Then several Lords etc, crowds of film stars Michael Wilding, John Mills, Trevor Howard, Laurence Olivier, Vivien Leigh, Robert Morley. I went into the ball of death (a circus performance) alongside Prince Ali Khan. All the shows, roundabouts, and fairground stalls were free and you could win all sorts of things. The boating lake had a huge balloon, the one they fly up in, in the film, hanging over it. Geoff and I went sailing with a glass of champagne each. There was a wonderful dance with the floor right next to the lake and beautiful lights and flowers everywhere. There was a gigantic fireworks display over the lake, huge jeroboams of champagne from Paris, but the best of all, really incredible restaurants. The food was from all different countries in the world, hot Indian curries, Chinese and Japanese rice dishes, American foods, English, German, French, Italian, everything. Each different country had a separate pavilion where they served and all the people serving were wearing the clothes of that country. We looked all-round and finally settled on Virginia ham, we must have had one pound each, all stuck with spices and cloves and served with peaches and pineapple, better than I have ever tasted in the US. It just makes my mouth water, as I never tasted such delicious food. We went to India for our sweet course, I had a wonderful thing of basically strawberries and cream and Geoff had lots of different cakes, and then we had the Indian ice cream, tasting like melons. There were any drinks you wanted to have, any wines you wanted, it really was like a dream. We met George Weidenfeld, Felix and Anthea were there too. Felix got us the tickets by a real stroke of luck, as Geoff had been writing for architecture magazines. It cost Mike Todd 75,000 pounds so you can imagine how lavish it was.

It was quite light in the morning when we were leaving on the river and everything was wonderful, with the mist hanging over the river. Todd took us all back to town in the boats, where we picked up our car. It was about seven o'clock when I got into bed so I'm feeling very tired now! I do wish you could have seen how beautiful everything was. I can't believe I ever went!

Spencer House was still getting improvements all the time. Felix and Anthea's five-year lease was up in 1961, and they moved over to Lindsey House in Blackheath Village. Their flat, was taken, by David and Darryl Morgan. They had just come back to London from Singapore, he was English and had been a rubber planter in Singapore, and had met Darryl who was from Perth, Australia. She was very tall, blond and very stunning looking, and David was starting an advertising company in England. They had the whole flat completely redone, new kitchen, new carpets, new curtains, and new bathroom fixtures. We gave them a five-year lease so that it was worth their while.

Darryl got a very good job in the new Time Life offices she was the glamour girl sitting at the front desk as a receptionist. We were always very amused, as Darryl had an amazing tan, having lived in Australia and Singapore, and as soon as our sun came out she would go into the garden in her bikini with some shiny reflective metallic faced panels, and lie down with all the reflected sun angled onto her as well as the real direct sun. She always kept her tan even in our English climate.

Very often in the summer when we got hot weather, we would think how lovely it would be if we could get to a beach, or somewhere to swim, but all the roads out of London were so full on those summer weekends, so David Morgan suggested we dig a pool in our garden. It was a very large garden so a pool would not be too disruptive an element. We got picks and shovels and started digging by hand; there was no way to take any mechanical equipment in, as it was a complete walled garden. We started in the winter and we had to carry all the excavated earth through at the side of the house, and have it picked up every Monday morning from the pavement in front of Spencer House.

By Easter we had the pool dug out, and I got a concrete firm in to do the bottom concrete slab, we had set the drain in the lowest point and connected it with a large pipe which ran up to the filter unit.

Once the slab was in, I got bricks delivered and built a 9 inch wall on all four sides in brick, with the water pipes incoming and outgoing through the bricks. At the back of my wall I poured concrete in as it went up, so that the water pressure wouldn't crack my wall, we had done a very clean cut through the dirt and had not disturbed the sides as we dug down. When the brickwork was complete we got the firm Geoff was using on Sanderson's to tank (waterproof) their basements, to do a smooth stucco waterproof finish inside the pool. I capped the wall with non-slip tiles. Then it was all ready for filling with water and testing it out, it was so refreshing to plunge in after a sticky hot day, and David used to do several lengths before work in the morning. We never got any cracks it was a great success. In the freezing weather we would float a log in it, so the ice pressure would not crack the stucco. It is not good in the frost to have a pool empty. For a while we left it unpainted, but after a year or two painted it in a rubber base swimming pool paint.

Sarah and Nils could swim by the time we had it completed, and Tanya wore little arm bands, they had such fun with it, on cold days they had an inflatable dingy, and when it rained they wore their yellow fishermen's type raincoats and sou'westers to row around. Geoff and I designed a great Pool house, with a wall of glass facing the pool, and we had a building firm to do that. I still had some old bricks left from the wall at the front of the house, so I built two brick walls coming out at right angles to the garden wall, and then the elegant glass front went in between them. In front of the pool house we laid a brick terrace, and on the other side we had a large wooden deck, which was a great spot to lie on, and got the last rays of afternoon sun.

We were at a party one night and I was chatting to someone who turned out to be a reporter, and I had told him about my project so he sent someone round to photograph me at work and he wrote it all up.

Darryl in the meantime had had a little boy, and David's business was so successful so he decided to sell it and they moved to Perth Australia. He started a building development company and I guess built blocks of high-rise apartments and hotels in Perth. We kept in touch for years, and when we were in San Luis Obispo, California, in 1970 they telephoned me and asked if I would book them into the Madonna Inn, it was even famous out in Perth! It was very good to see them both again. A few years later I telephoned them and David had the sad news that Darryl had been killed in a head-on collision. She had come out of her yoga class, and been driving on the wrong side of the road. David was bringing up their two boys.

Sarah and Nils were at Brooklands School in Blackheath Village. It was a fairly good school, as it was a real mixture of professional families children and working class from the estate near there. The one poor aspect of the school was the headmistress, who was very religious. I had bad experience, from the convent school, about religion and tried not to influence the children's straightforward logical thinking, by confusing their brains with illogical religious beliefs.

When Sarah was at Brooklands School, one day she asked me did I know what made my seeds in the garden grow. She said 'God makes them grow.' I felt so cross as I had tried to stick to logical explanations, I said God couldn't make them grow unless I planted them and then kept them watered, so in fact it was me that made them grow.

Nils and later Tanya had gone for a short time to a little pre-school with Mrs. Thomas but Nils hadn't enjoyed it much, and cried each day when I left him. Maxine was in his little school, but that didn't cheer him up. Once the children got into Brooklands School we met a lot of local people, architects etc. Walter and Glen Bor had a little girl Kathy, who was a good friend of Sarah's. Walter was from Czechoslovakia and was a town planner, first in the LCC and later in Liverpool, and then in private practice with Sir Llewelyn Davies.

Glen was Welsh, and they had an amazing vacation cottage in Wales, which I loved to take the children to. It was a very old stone place, I think it had been a rectory originally, and was at least 15 miles from the nearest house or road, in the middle of a Forestry preserve. It had no electricity and no water and I found it was very satisfying to be able to survive without the modern amenities and with no shops available. It proved we could still live independently of all the modern amenities.

Walter used to say just bring a few eggs, and when we got there we went long hikes, coming back with amazing species of fungi. Walter had lived on these in the war in Czechoslovakia, and knew which ones you could eat safely. We got so many, so he dried them in the sun. There were all kinds of berries to eat too. It was a very rigorous and strict way of living. Every morning we walked down through the woods to a good stream, and there we got big bags of drinking water for everyone to carry back to the house. We stood in the river and poured the river water over us to clean us up, and brushed our teeth down there too. We never seem to have heard of giardia! Everyone had an early morning job to do, someone had to dig a trench to empty the toilet into, another person had to trim the oil lamps and refill them, and we had to collect firewood each day to burn on a wonderful cast iron stove which was in the kitchen fireplace. It had an iron tank at the side of the fire and we filled it with water so we always had some hot water to do dishes. It had a grate to lower over the fire and you did the cooking on that. I thought it was a wonderful relaxing holiday, but Geoffrey only came once, and he hated it!

In the late 60's when we lived in Albuquerque, New Mexico, we visited several communes in that area, and they were all such disasters, and later had to be closed down by the health authorities. Walter Bor had such sensible ideas for disciplining all of us to keep a healthy environment, water was boiled, and toilets were emptied and buried every day. In the Hippie 60's no one had any idea what was involved in planning a daily routine for a group, and keeping up any hygienic standard. The slopes of a hill at one of the communes had sewage seeping from hopelessly constructed sanitation, running down, and the small children and dogs were all sick to their stomachs. All the hippies sat with flowers in their hair discussing airhead ideas all day. We went to a commune that had two locations, one for summer in the mountains, and another they went to in the fall, for the winter, in the valley on lower ground. The weekend we went, they had just moved to the mountain location, and when it got to mid afternoon they suddenly realised it was lunch time, so looking at me as the only person who looked at all practical, they asked me to go and make some peanut butter sandwiches. When I went into the room supposed to be a kitchen, I found everything had been left out from the previous Fall. The only knife was all caked up with old dried food and almost impossible to get it clean. Luckily they got closed down before anyone died.

When Tanya was four she started at Mrs. Thomas's pre-school, and about that time I heard that Lewisham Council wanted architects to propose a scheme for the New Town Hall. The old town hall was stone, but very dirty and ugly and old, it was in the centre of a traffic island and so got all the dirt and dust from the buses and cars going around it. The council members were going to interview architects and I was one of them. I took some of my old drawings in and explained I had been at home with three children since 1955, so had no recent schemes, but my proposal for the Town Hall would be to have a glass and stainless steel curtain wall building, that could have the structural elements outside, all cleaned with the windows every six months, and kept looking new and shining something to be proud of. After the interview we all sat in one room, and the guys were all bragging about their ideas and seemed to be confident they would be chosen. Suddenly it was announced from the council chamber that June Holroyd was to go back in—I thought they were going to ask me more questions, but all the guys in the room got up and left, I guess they realised that I had got the job.

When I got home it gradually dawned on me what I had taken on, I wondered how I could possibly manage with the house to run, and three small children. I started to look around for a full-time live-in housekeeper, so I would be able to concentrate on what seemed a huge job, especially when I had had several years at home with the children. I found an older person in The Lady magazine, probably in her late fifties, Miss Whatley. She had been with an English family in Canada and had good references.

I had not had any office type of clothes since 1955 (when I had Sarah) so I had to go out and get a complete new wardrobe. I was to have an office in Lewisham Town Hall, but I would have some freedom of my hours as I was working on my own.

The whole architecture department in the town hall was a very weird untalented set up. The man in charge was an old chap called Mr. Forward. He had not trained as an architect, he had got in as a licentiate, they were architects who had never studied Architecture at a University or architecture school, but had worked in an architects office for several years, and got some sort of recognition for it (there were no architects in the office!) He had done a scheme for a new town hall several years before the war, but they could not get it passed, and could not get financing from the LCC. His name should have been Backward, not Forward. He was hopeless.

The town clerk was an extremely intelligent and sympathetic man, and he became my ally. He said I was like a breath of fresh air in the architecture department. I think he and one old chap from the Fire Dept. were the people on the committee who had voted for me.

I gradually got a scheme that seemed to work. My building was to be mainly a large new council chamber, and then small committee rooms and lounges for members. The interior of the council chamber I asked Hille furniture people to design the seating and desks etc. we planned an electric voting system which they had never had. I used a lot of white marble but detailed it in a very modern way, like Skidmore Owings and Merrill was doing in the USA. Mr. Forward said he had never seen marble detailed like that, and he gradually started to interfere. Geoffrey said let him do the council chamber interior and you do the rest. I worked on it all for almost two years, and got all the working drawings done. I made a model of the whole group of Town Hall buildings and my new building, and I gave several slide shows to the committee and I won them over, but Mr. Forward was a real pain, couldn't stop meddling with my scheme, although I was not working under him.

Miss Whatley was a very good housekeeper but was not vaguely sensitive or artistic, and when the children came in from school with all their paintings and drawings to show us, she just tidied everything away. When I got in from work, she had all three children bathed and well scrubbed and dinner on the way, she would pour me a sherry and keep me out of her kitchen, as she thought I used her clean tea towels to take things out of the oven!! Meals always had to be on time—she was very inflexible. After dinner I often had to return to the office for another hour or two of work. The model took me a long time to complete, so that was done mainly in the evenings, when it was all quiet in the town hall.

On Sundays Miss Whatley always cooked a big lunch, which had to be eaten at 1pm and we were often asked out for drinks on Sunday mornings and she couldn't push lunchtime to 2pm! She also cooked us lots of bread and butter puddings (she was very thrifty and I think couldn't bear to throw any bread away) and Geoff kept asking her for ice cream, we were not used to cooked puddings. I had had them always at home and boarding school when I was young and I liked them,—they are a very English thing, treacle sponge with custard is still one of my favorites, though I never make it. I could gradually see my elegant town hall building being chipped away, and the children were not enjoying the new household routine too much, so I resigned. The Town Clerk was terribly sad when I went to say goodbye, he and I were kindred spirits. I thought that as Mr. Forward seemed to dislike any modern design, that they would probably throw all my drawings into the trash, when I left. I never heard from anyone what was happening to it.

One of the days while I was working on my Town Hall I was about to go to a very critical meeting with the committee, when Miss Whatley telephoned to ask me to go home immediately as Nils had done a handstand on a window sill two floors up with the window open, and over balanced and landed on the top of his head. He needed taking to hospital, so I dropped everything and rushed home. Tanya had apparently dared him to do a handstand he said, and he had landed on concrete and split the skin on the top of his head! I realised then that mothers that work have tremendous drawbacks, they had never thought to phone Geoff—and of course he couldn't drive—perhaps nowadays it might be different.

I decided it was a much more satisfying life to have children and be working from home. We got a new au pair girl, Ingerlise from Copenhagen, a very sweet girl and one of our happiest ones. In the fall of 1964 I got pregnant again and planned to have two more children as I always found them such a joy.

Just after I found I was pregnant, we were already booked to go to Egypt for a winter vacation. Before we left I telephoned Mrs. Rowe, my old midwife, to tell her I would be needing her again the following May, she said she had retired, but as she had been a midwife for my other babies, she would come back to me, but she added if you're just off to Egypt, you won't be pregnant when you get back. I wondered why she said that?

Anyway we had a great holiday, Tanya went with Ingerlise, our Danish au pair, to Mummy's and Sarah and Nils stayed with friends in London. We flew to Cairo and went to Sakhara and Cheops and to all the amazing mosques in the City. Egypt was in a very primitive state, Nasser had given everybody a little portable radio, as many people could not read papers, and were very uneducated, and on Friday mornings he broadcast a long talk to the whole country, trying to get them to think in a more modern way. He talked one morning about all the diseases they were getting from flies. Everywhere was so dirty and flies covered everything. In the morning when we came out of our hotel there were women waiting for 'bakshish' they often carried a child with sores all over their faces and heads, covered in flies.

One of our taxi drivers was telling us he had several families, all very poor, but his religion told him that the worse this life was, it would be made up to him in the next one. I thought another crazy religion! He was heaping misery on himself and his many families thinking they would all be rewarded for eternity.

We left Cairo to go down to Luxor and the Valley of the Kings. That was an amazing experience. We had booked a hotel in Luxor, but when we arrived we found they were still building it. Such cock-eyed building work too. The workmen were wearing pyjamas and wandering back and forth with baskets carrying some cement or concrete. They had some rooms just about done, so we had one of those. Each time we used an appliance like the shower, the handle fell off, and light switches were not properly attached and fell on the floor. They were lacking any one who could direct them, and who knew how the appliances should work, or someone who had ever seen the modern appliances before.

There were a group of Engineers, Egyptians, trained by the government who were working on the Aswan Dam and they would come up to Luxor to escape on weekends. Because the government had trained them they had to work there for five years, but after that, they all planned to leave and go to Europe and look for work in Germany, as they said it was impossible to get anything properly built. Poor Nasser, it seemed he was fighting a losing battle. We had gone to the Engineering Office for the Aswan Dam whilst we were in Cairo, (that in itself was an unbelievable place, they had an elevator in the building but it had people living in it and other people living on the roof of the elevator) as we had hoped to visit Abu Simbel, but they were in the process of moving it all to higher ground, so we could not have seen anything.

(I must just add a note here about the amazing incident that has just happened in Egypt. It is now February 11ᵗʰ 2011, we have just witnessed the Egyptians finally being able to rid themselves of the dictator in power, Hosni Mubarek. It was the result of an uprising,

a very peaceful one, by the millions of Egyptians in Cairo, Suez and Alexandria.

They are hoping to turn the politics into a Democracy. They have been under a Dictator for six thousand years. Recently we have all seen China escape to become a very successful economy under a communist rule, but they have gone from a very peasant society, to being in competition with the top world economies. All the young people have ipods now and see Twitter and hear how some parts of the world mainly China have had phenomenal leaps forward.

Egypt had a corrupt royal family that amassed great wealth, Nasser was in the Egyptian Army and the army took over the country and the Royal Family all moved to wealthy areas round the world. Luckily the people are not violent, and this seizing of the power was done very peacefully. They now have to get some agreement on a plan to get a voting system to work, so they can all vote for their next President. They have suffered from being held back by tyrannical leaders. The last thirty years they have suffered under Mubareck. We wish them a very secure future, and hope they can vote for a good form of Government, and safeguard themselves from the corruption that they have in Lebanon with their Hamas rulers.)

Anyway the things we had come to see were fantastic. It was such really powerful architecture, and quite unbelievably skilled artifacts. The big temple in Luxor, we visited frequently, as we were staying near there. We were amazed by the scale of the columns, and the remains of the original painted decoration. Each morning when we came out of the hotel we took a felucca across the River Nile to the Valley of the Kings. The boat was always full of Egyptians, almost like they were waiting for us. On our last evening I was complaining to a tourist office manager in our hotel, how expensive the ride across the Nile was, and when I told him what we had paid, he said we had paid for the whole boat! Everyone had been waiting for a free ride when we arrived!

When we got off the felucca on the other side, there was a guide selling tickets to visit the tombs, and we said we wanted to see all the tombs so we paid for the ticket, which included everything. When we got to each tomb entrance there was another guy in his pyjamas, wanting more money to go in, I argued with them that we had paid for everything, but it was no good, as we needed to have a series of guys reflecting the light into the tombs for us. There was no electric light, so the first chap standing outside with a mirror shone the sunlight to the first corner, where another chap stood and caught the light and directed the light to the next man's mirror, and so on right into the centre of the tomb, we were dependent on them all!

They crowded around us hoping to sell us all kinds of scarab beetles and little carved figures. We were there not long after the Suez Crisis, so they had had a period with no tourists to live off, so I think we had a worse time than usual.

The people in that area have always lived off the tombs of the Pharoes. The tombs had been built and later plundered by their ancestors. as they had worked for the Pharoes, they knew their way into the tombs and the treasures. When Flinders Petrie and all the German archaeologists had taken groups over to excavate new tombs and treasures, these local people had provided the labour, and we heard that they would dig away for nine months or even a year, but when they noticed the Europeans were despairing of ever finding anything else, and were likely to give up and return home, the locals would suddenly produce some treasure which would get the archaeologists enthusiastic again, for another long period of exploration.

The large tombs were really incredible inside, with the walls and ceilings covered with wall paintings and so vast, rooms after rooms. Tutankhaman's tomb with the outer mummy case still in place and the decorated furniture and walls, it was hard to believe that the ancestors of the local people had been capable of such fine work.

The noblemen's tombs are on a much smaller scale, scattered around the West Bank of the Nile, and had a very small entrance to squeeze in, some of those I let Geoff go in on his own, as they looked claustrophobic, but the ones I saw had a main chamber which was covered with illustrations of the nobleman's life at the time they had died, with scenes of fishing on flat bottomed boats on the Nile river, playing with children, and gathering fruit, they were wonderful records of their daily life.

There were two very nice Dutch people staying in our hotel, and we all four wanted to visit Dendera, the temple of the Godess Hathor. We shared a rented car with a driver with them, and drove all along the banks of the Nile to Dendera. It was like going back to biblical times, people were all out working the fertile strip of land around the Nile, and they had long poles that were supported on a tripod sort of leg, with a leather bag on the end, which they dipped into the Nile and filled with water and then they swung the bag round to the higher level and then the next person did the same it was like a series of ladders to get the water up to the higher ground. It was an amazing drive.

We spent a long time in the Temple of Hathor (goddess of love) it is a huge place and had a very unusual level above the main temple, which was only for the priests. One stone room had the entire ceiling carved with the figure of Hathor goddess of love with large breasts hanging down, the whole ceiling was this one figure. I am not sure what ceremony the priests did in there.

On our return journey it was already dark and our car broke down in a little village. In the evening after dark all the women were allowed out and they were all completely in black. We got a crowd of the pyjama clad men poking their heads in our engine, they looked like they had never seen a car before. But finally they got it going, and we went off back to Luxor. I think that was the night that all the women came out wailing all night on the banks of the Nile. A child had been swept away in the Nile waters. It runs very fast and they all kept standing in the edges near the bank, to wash their faces and under their robes before the Muezzin. There were cows in the edge too and the locals were all washing out their mouths in this dirty looking water. There is a parasite worm in the Nile that gets into peoples flesh, poor Nasser, he had a long way to go with his hygiene lectures.

Many people had no house, but lived simply under a large tree for shade and had to protect themselves with rifles, because at night the Bedouins from the desert, occasionally swept down and robbed the Egyptians living along the Nile, of their animals, crops and their few possessions.

When we got back to Cairo we spent a whole day in the large museum there and it had wonderful treasures, which were found in the Valley of the King's. I remember a sculpture of a little dwarf man and a much larger woman who had her arm around his shoulders they were man and wife, and apparently there was no prejudice against deformities. We also went up north to Alexandria on the Mediterranean. It seemed a much more modern City, I swam in the sea there. We returned to Cairo to fly home.

It is quite an extraordinary sight to see Egypt from the air, just the one strip of green following the Nile and then vast deserts beyond that. At the mouth of the Nile, where it empties into the Mediterranean there were long lines of muddy water mixing into the sea, like an extraordinary painting.

As soon as we were back in London I phoned Mrs. Rowe and said after all the camel rides etc. I was still pregnant and she was amazed. She said when she was a young girl she had gone out on the dig with the Flinders Petrie's expedition, her job had been piecing remnants of pottery together, and I guess everyone had got pretty sick from the water and food.

Soon after our holiday in Egypt we decided to remodel the large salon, the old ballroom. We discovered we had enough height to have a two storey section, and we thought it would make a wonderful room for Geoffrey and me to use, and try to keep the children and toys out, so we would always have one special room for visitors and grownups. The three children, Sarah, Nils and Tanya were all sleeping in the large salon and they had a theatre stage and a huge garden slide and a swing and all their toys, and a piano in there. It had worked very well as a big nursery for them, while they were very young.

We had had a bedroom around at the front of the house since we moved in, and the room next to it was our living room, the one I had first fixed up. We had the au pair girls room which we left as it was, and then the children's living room, which opened on to the garden. Geoffrey and I did a scheme for the big room, and got a very good firm of shop fitters, who did Simpson's on Piccadilly, to do all the construction. As the room had a very good plaster cornice, all perfectly intact, we kept our structure free of that. The whole balcony support was one long 'I' beam, which they brought in from the back garden, through one of the large windows.

It was a really beautiful and elegant scheme. We used all modern materials, satin finished aluminium for handrails, on the balcony and stairs. The panels were white with black ebonised wood edges and the stairs, desk and shelves were in Canadian pine.

We were very excited to get it done but we only just got it completed, when my new baby was due. The contractors had planned for the baby's arrival (which was supposed to be late in May) as their deadline, but of course when it was completed we had the entire house to move around! Sarah went into our old bedroom, at the front of the house, Tanya moved into the room next to hers, which had been our living room, and Nils took over the old children's living room with big French doors onto the garden.

Both Sarah and Nils were afraid at first, in their rooms. We had had so much trouble with burglars. There were some steps into Perceval house next door, that made it possible for someone to step across on to the window sill in what had been our bedroom, so Sarah was afraid of that, and Nils' room with French doors opening onto the big garden was also scary for him.

We had had a number of people breaking in to our ground floor flat. One evening when Geoff was still up in town, and our au pair girl was out, I was sitting eating dinner on my own in the kitchen when I saw a shadow go down the hall, when I went out it was a young guy who said he was looking for his pals, the painters. I was so furious with him, and told him I did all the painting. I asked him to show me how he had got in. In the big salon room there was the same problem with steps into the back of Perceval House and he had stepped across the wide area in front of the basement windows, where Nils had tumbled down, and he had pushed open one of our bottom sash windows, so I got the bottom part of the sash windows, those on the front and back of the house permanently closed. You could still pull the top sash down for air, as it was too high for someone to climb over it After he climbed out I phoned the police as I realized he had been a burglar. Robbery was a way of life for a lot of London lads at that time.

Another night about 4am the police telephoned to say they had a young boy who they had caught in my car, they had him at the police station in Deptford, and he had told them I had lent him my car. They came up to pick me up and take me down to see if I could identify him—of course I couldn't. He had cut the canvas top of our lovely little Morris car, to open the door and then had hotwired it or something. The policeman on duty said to me I should buy a crook lock, which locked the accelerator pedal to the steering wheel. Even with that device the car went again, they had managed to break the Crook Lock and the car was found abandoned in another suburb, minus its radio. This time it was another police guy and he said, to get something much more difficult to cut through, so I got a very big thick chain and padlocked the car each night. Sure enough it went again. This time another policeman told me the big chain had been a bad idea, as it issued a challenge to these guys, which they could not resist!

We got a bigger car, an American Ford convertible, as our family had outgrown the Morris minors, (we had had two of them-and we loved them) with the new car I had a burglar alarm built in, I had to turn a key to set it each time. Some nights the wind would rock the car and set it off, and other nights the local yobs would give it a push as they went past. We slept at the front of the house and for a while it used to wake me up, but I got to the stage that I slept through it.

One year, just before Christmas I went up to town to do some shopping for presents for the children, and came back in time to take the presents into the house, and then go off immediately to meet them across Blackheath, as they came out of school (I had to do this every single day which was really a bore) so I locked the car, it was my big Ford, and set the alarm, went in and put the presents into my cupboard and came straight out, and there were still the wet tire tread marks on the road, but no sign of the car. This was in broad daylight. Some friends were walking up the hill from Lewisham station and they said they had just seen the mechanic driving my car like crazy, down the hill to Lewisham with the burglar alarm going! The guy was wearing a white overall, like mechanics wore. That time we were without the car for about a week, and when it was found in North London it had been used for a bank robbery, and they had messed about with the engine, I guess to hot it up. Their tools for breaking in places, were in my boot, (trunk) and a huge bunch of keys, there must have been hundreds. They had apparently been caught at the Bank, but my car had just been left. Again another trip to the police station in North London to get the car and to say that all the jemmies and keys in the back were not mine! They had wrecked my clutch, so I had to get that repaired. It was so difficult living where we did without a car, and three children needing to go to school, dancing, and riding lessons and to see friends, it began to drive me crazy.

I was sitting in the children's lounge one summer evening with the French doors open, before Nils moved in to that room, reading the Sunday papers, suddenly there were three idiot boys with their heads through the door from the garden—I said 'What the hell are you doing there?' and they said isn't this the house for sale? They were always such cheeky cockney lads and they always had a smart answer. There was nowhere to get into the back garden as we had a big locked gate built, at the side of the house, but I think they came through the entrance hall of Perceval house, and then came over into our garden.

We had a pub at the end of Dartmouth Row on the main A2, Dover Road. A lot of the car theft was because when the pub closed there was no bus to take them to Lewisham or Lee Green, in fact most of the bus routes had stopped by that hour. They just saw our convertibles as a way to get home.

Another time we were all sitting at the end of the garden, in the afternoon sun, and we had some friends round for tea. I went in with the au pair girl to make the tea, and she tried to pop into her room, but the door was locked from the inside, we went out to tell the others and when we came back we noticed her window was wide open and the guy had obviously jumped out and had left her door locked. He had grabbed her purse and a small radio. We had not been able to see him, as we had the sun in our eyes, sitting at the far end of the garden.

For a Christmas present one year we bought Nils a lovely go-cart, it was one you peddle, not motorized, and he used to take it over to the hollows on Blackheath, near to us, and drive it up and down the big slopes. He came back for tea one-day and just as we sat down I said to Nils 'Did you put your go cart through the side gate?' He ran to the front door, and already it had gone! We never saw it again.

One night when Geoff and I were asleep in the front bedroom of the house, there were suddenly lights flashing into our room, and people talking in the front garden, so I opened the window and they said it was the police and they were looking for some prowlers. I went out of the garden doors into the back garden, and saw my big garden fork leaning on the wall, I grabbed it and ran down the garden—after all these thefts I think I would have killed the prowlers—but luckily I didn't find them!

Later we had a couple of burglaries upstairs as the folk were out all day, so I got an electrical firm in, to install one of the front door Electric locks, like the one we had had in Boston USA. You will get the feeling that Londoners are a bunch of thieves, and I guess they really are. The one thing that was not too bad, they were not really scary people. They never carried guns and always seemed to have a good sense of humour, but of course for children it was very worrying.

Children always seem to develop fears though, when we lived in the centre of London, Sarah and I always used to go to the park, Russell Square or Coram's Fields, and she crawled on the grass and ate leaves etc. but we never did any digging in the soil. When we got to Spencer House and I was always gardening, I bought Sarah a little set of tools, but she was horrified to find worms in the soil. She had bad dreams and said the worms were getting under her door; she was in the room with french doors onto the garden. Later she was afraid of a lovely big owl who used to sit on a branch of a huge cherry tree, next to the nursery window and watch them playing. He was very beautiful, but inquisitive.

My fourth baby had been due in late May, but the doctor said it could come any minute, and as the other births had been so quick, he didn't want me to go far from home. I had taken my castor oil on a Friday night, but it did not have any effect. Finally on June 26th about 4 weeks late, I had a baby boy. We were all so delighted with him, especially Sarah who was old enough to really help me to look after him. We still had our very sweet au pair girl, Ingerlise from Copenhagen, and my parents came down again and I think they stayed at Lydia House, round the corner on the heath. It was wonderful to be in our very elegant new room, I moved a single bed on the main floor so I was facing our whole new balcony section. The upper part of the balcony was our new bedroom with the big bed in it, but as everyone wanted to pop in and see the baby, I was best on the lower floor.

Geoffrey went to the library once again and came back armed with all the dictionaries of names, and was busy thinking of trendy London names, and we really couldn't agree on one. Nils' friends had typical London names—Inigo, Rupert, Marius, and Aaron, some poor boys were called Tarquin and a friend of ours has just called their little boy Titus. I always think how many times they will have to defend their names in school. In England we have six weeks before you have to register the name, but now the time was up and we still had not been able to agree on a name, so I went down to the registry office with a list of strange fancy names, Geoff said just pick one, I suddenly decided to call him Sam, and his second name Benedict. When Geoff came home and I told him, he said it wasn't even on our list! It has suited him so well all tese years, a good, down-to-earth name, so I think it was a good choice. But I remember in the 70's America, Sam said to me," The only Sams I know are all dogs!!"

After Sam was born, I decided it was the perfect time to take up flying lessons. I had always dreamed I could fly and ever since Daddy had stopped me training as a ferry pilot in the war, I wanted to ferry (deliver) planes from the US to Britain, I had been longing to start flying. He said ferry planes were shot down all the time, it was too dangerous and as he put it "I don't want to just throw away all your expensive education". Here is a great picture, from my first book, of the two of us 'thick as thieves'.

Blackheath where we lived was not far away from Biggin Hill, which had been a very well known airfield in the defense of London in the war, and had wonderful associations with all the great spitfire pilots from the 'Battle of Britain 'days.

I drove out there one day, and found it was very simple to enroll for lessons. The plane I was to fly was a German 'Bolkow' from Munich. My instructor was a very sweet man from India. The plane had wonderful visibility, a curved glass dome that clipped down over us, so we had a 360degree view of everything. London had very strict rules for these small private planes, there was an inverted cone shaped area over London, which was purely for commercial planes to use, but when you got out to the suburbs the ceiling for private planes gradually got higher.

It was all so simple then, we had no radio or contact with control towers, and we had a lot of maps that were virtually road maps, we would start out from London following the A2 road down to the south coast, and then fly out over the 'white cliffs of Dover' and over the Channel. It was so beautiful visually, like your wildest dream. One day as we were leaving the London area I asked my instructor if we could fly low over Blackheath and Greenwich, we could see Spencer House clearly and even see Sam's pram in the back garden!

There were some very exciting lessons to learn, putting the plane into too steep a climb, so that the stall warning started flashing and hooting, and then the engine cut out and the nose of the plane started to drop, and for a moment that dive was something you felt was so exciting you could go all the way down, but then you had to keep calm and restart the engine and gradually pull the nose up. All the steep banking turns were very exciting too. I had to have medical check-ups all the time to fly, but it had always been my dream, so was well worth it. Daddy would telephone me to tell me how crazy I was with four children to be taking such risks. I guess his generation never felt very confident about flying.

Later in that year, 1965, Geoff was invited by MIT and the architecture school in St. Louis, and the Institute of Design in Chicago to go over and give lectures, so we (just Geoff and I) decided to return in Spring 1966 and we flew back to the States. We stayed with Thais on Francis Avenue in Cambridge Mass, and saw Mrs. Brinnin too. Thais gave a nice dinner party for some of our old friends. We flew from there on to St. Louis where we didn't really know anyone so we stayed in a hotel. I remember one of the faculty took us out to dinner to a new gaslight area on the river. They were busy knocking down all the wonderful picturesque old Wharf buildings that had so much character, and were replacing them with cheaply constructed false faced type buildings. I was very upset at how much new building in the US was being built the same way. The detail and craftsmanship in the old buildings can never be replaced, as so few people have those skills, and even if they do, very few people can afford to pay for the time involved to produce really good buildings, with hand crafted details.

America did seem to be in a much happier state though, than in the early 1950s when we had all the witch hunting and Mc.Carthy persecutions. We stayed with John and Jano Walley, in Chicago, and in spite of keeping in touch by letters all those years, we really had become very far apart, and didn't have much in common any more. Geoffrey and I both felt very sad to discover that, I think Geoffrey has always thought that letter writing does not give you a good picture of the other person, and in the case of John and Jano, it was certainly true.

They had moved from 6 East Kinzie St. further north, and had a wonderful big high studio. A few years later we heard from Jano, that John had been on the top of a high ladder in the studio and had fallen off and been killed. We were very sad to hear this, as he had been an outstanding person, and a wonderful friend, so generous with his time and introducing us to so many interesting friends when we had lived in Chicago in the 50's. (All in my first book.)

On that same trip we went to Los Angeles to see Charles and Ray Eames, as Geoffrey and Peter and Allison Smithson were doing a whole issue of Architectural Design about them. They were both highly talented designers. They left a legacy of very innovative chair designs, they made amazing short films, and had designed a very well known house for themselves on the bluff in Santa Monica. Geoffrey had written about their work in 1953, but there was suddenly a lot of interest in them in the mid—Sixties. After the issue of Architectural Design came out in England, Charles Eames came over to England and visited the AA. where Geoff was teaching. Monica Pigeon who was the editor of Architectural Design, and one or two other people suggested Geoff should really do a book about the Eames and their work.

After Sandersons was completed, Geoffrey was asked, by a developer from Scotland who had just bought Gorringes department store in Victoria, London, to design a shopping centre in Watford. There were no shopping centres in England at that time, so it was a very exciting project. After months and months of work many of the small shopkeepers in the Watford area started a public inquiry as they thought it would take business away from them. I'd think actually it would have helped their business as Watford is on the London end of the A1 motorway, so people from all around that area would have come to Watford to shop. Geoff and the developer attended lots of sessions in Court, on the public inquiry, and the final result was, that it was all stopped.

I hated to see Geoff's disappointment and waste of all his work, England has always been very slow at accepting new ideas, especially from the States, but now they have some of the biggest shopping centres in the world, 40 years later!!

Geoff decided in the spring of 1967 to go to America to collect material for his book on the Eames. I thought if he was going, we should all go. After our earlier stay in the 50's I was very apprehensive about taking all of us away from England, but our trip in 1965 had been a better experience of the States, and once Geoffrey and I were separated for a long period, chances are he would have been snapped up by some of the desperate divorced ladies looking for a new man!

If we were all going I suddenly had a lot of work to do. We realised we would need to find a job for Geoff to support us all. He had been enjoying teaching at the Architecture Association in London, and through them, we heard that Tim Vreeland at the University of New Mexico was looking for an architect to teach there in Albuquerque, so although that was not in California near the Eames, we decided at such short notice, we would not find anything nearer, so that began to take shape, and Jean Vreeland, Tim's wife said she would find a house for us in Albuquerque.

We had to find someone to take our flat in Spencer House and also a real estate company to run the other flats for me, so I found some real estate agents in Blackheath Village that would do that. I wrote a very detailed careful inventory of everything in our flat as apart from our clothes, we were leaving it all behind.

Tanya, who was only eight years old, had been asked by Caroline and Nick Hill who had two boys Rupert and Marius, who were great friends of hers, to go with them for a month to the Dordogne in France, where they had a large house. We decided as our trip was still up in the air and seemed uncertain, that she should go.

Everything suddenly started to fall into place after they had left, we got confirmation on the job, and the house, and the US embassy wanted all the family to go in and get our immigrant visas set up, and have our medicals, and as Tanya was away we postponed it as long as we could. I wrote to Caroline and Nick and asked them if they could put Tanya on a plane or train, as we were hoping to leave on September first. We went off up to Sheffield to have a last visit with all the family, and say goodbye to them.

It began to get so near the time for us to leave, I got quite desperate, I sent a couple of telegrams to Nick and Caroline, and as they had no phone, I telephoned the village policeman and asked him to see what, if anything, they were planning. Tanya said she remembered all the activity of people on bicycles coming up with telegrams. The day before we were due to leave they came strolling back, Caroline and her husband Nick were both very impractical, and said "we knew we would be back before you left" but of course Tanya had no chance to say goodbye to anyone, and Geoff set straight out for the US Embassy in Grosvenor Square that afternoon, to take Tanya to get her green card set up—What a mess!!

I had bought a great new camera so we could get some good photos while we were away, and we had so much hand luggage, each of us had 2 pieces we were responsible for. We were flying Pan Am to Boston as Thais wanted us to visit her, and break the long flight. We had to take a small bus out to the planes at Heathrow, and we checked everyone's 2 pieces of hand luggage, but when we got in our seats on the plane Geoff had already lost my new expensive camera, another impractical guy! I think he had left it on the bus. We never saw it again!

We were only thinking we would be gone for a year, until Geoff did his trips to the Eames in Santa Monica, and got the material for him to write the book. After our first trip for two years in 1952, I was not looking forward to going back! I had not enjoyed the politics and the witch hunting of that time and the roll of women in Architecture and business as a whole!

We Return to the USA, plus 4 Children, 1967

We flew into Boston airport and Thais was there to meet us all, and take us to her lovely house on Francis Avenue. John Kenneth Galbraith, Julia Child and her husband, and Jose Luis Sert, who was the head of architecture in Harvard, all lived on that street in Cambridge. Thais' house was at the end, as Francis Avenue is a cul-de-sac, so that side of the house was beautiful and quiet, but at the back of the house was Massachusetts Avenue, which was terribly noisy and I remember the weather was very hot and humid, as it was the beginning of September, the children woke up several nights because of the noise of the fire trucks, and the heat and also jet lag. We rented a car and went down for a few days to Cape Cod, which was very pretty and had an English sort of look and it was cooler and pleasantly relaxing for a holiday before we took off for Albuquerque.

Jean and Tim Vreeland met us at the airport, and took us out to a very nice house they had found for us, it belonged to some faculty who were off on sabbatical. It looked like an adobe and was within sight of the Sandia Mountains. It was all furnished as the owners were just away for one year, and anything we were short of, Jean seemed to find. She was extremely kind and helpful to us.

Our first job before we could do anything was to go out and buy a car. We went over to Lomas Street and test drove the new Ford Mustang convertible, they were such great looking cars and so well designed, but unfortunately they were too small for six of us, but then we found a Plymouth Barracuda fast back, which was perfect. On long trips all four children could lean back with their heads under the big glass window of the fast back, looking up at the stars.

The school that Sarah, Nils, and Tanya were to go to was just a short walk away, but the University of New Mexico campus was a little way off. Geoff has never driven, so I drove him down there each day, as ferrying 4 children, we really missed the public transport of England. Sam was only two and as he was still in diapers, the little nursery school wouldn't take him, so he and I had some really fun outings during that year. I got a programme of all the Indian dances and festivals at the various pueblos around, and Sam loved all the Indian dancing, I bought him the straps with bells on, to go round his ankles as he danced.

Our children were very noticeable in that area, every single child in the school had very black hair, they were all Mexican or Indian, and our three had very blond hair and very trendy London clothes. Nils and Sam only had shorts as that is what boys in England wear, and it was terribly hot, so it seemed to be sensible, but I should have found out what the other kids would be wearing, as they all had a very difficult time because they looked so different. I had forgotten how very conservative children are, and they want everyone to conform to them. I probably should have gone and bought the typical school clothes that everyone had, and got their hair cut very short, but I thought we were only there for a year, and I really loved the swinging clothes from London. Poor Sarah and Tanya had a very hard time as their dresses were very short minis and all the other girls' skirts were at or below their knees, like old ladies. Tanya's teacher was a real horror; she got Tanya in front of all the class to bend over so that everyone could see her underwear. I really can't stand that kind of abuse, especially from a teacher! I would have used the opportunity to open up the children's ideas a bit, and given them a chance to learn about clothes in other countries, you know open up their minds a little!

Geoff was teaching fifth year architecture students and he had some really interesting ones. Some we are still in touch with, quite a few were from the Indian pueblos. One of the brightest ones was

A. Thomas Torres (Tommy) we were all very fond of him. When he finished at U N M, he went to University of California, Berkeley and did a business course and has turned out to be a very bright businessman, he practices architecture down in Malibu, and he and Geoff have done quite a few building projects together.

Tim and Jean Vreeland, had two little girls, Daisy and Phoebe. Jean was very sweet. We had some lovely visits to their house, and parties. They had a big Halloween party for the children, all in fancy dress. Tim was from the East coast and his mother, Diana Vreeland who was the editor of Vogue, was very well known, so Tim got a lot of interesting visitors stopping off in Albuquerque to see him, and then he would ask us in for drinks or dinner to meet them.

He was friendly with Charles Moore, the well—known architect, and he stopped in a few times. We didn't feel too cut-off, as we were on people's route as they went from the East coast to the West. Walter Bor came to stay with us; he was our town planner friend who had the remote cottage in Wales. He really loved our area, and it was certainly another world from London, or anywhere in Europe. We took him up the aerial tramway to the top of the Sandia mountains, which were all snow covered and more than 6,000 feet and the view from there of what looked like a great desert below, all sandy and barren and hot.

We drove up to Taos with him and went to the Taos Indian pueblo, which is a very amazing group of adobe houses all piled on top of each other, with ladders for people to climb on the roof of some houses, to get up to their own house. Walter was a town planner, and I think he found Taos Pueblo very unusual. Walter was very dark and looked as if he could have been an Indian, he was very interested in everything, but surprised to find the Indians didn't want him to take a photo of them, or their pueblo. We went up to Santa Fe many times, it was only an hour or so drive and was such a pretty town compared to Albuquerque, which was laid out on a grid and apart from a few old buildings in the old downtown square, it was not very beautiful.

The Rio Grande had no water as it went through Albuquerque. We visited Corrales and found that was our nearest interesting place, the Centerline Store there had some really great things.

Just after we arrived in Albuquerque there was a big State Fair and people came from all over the area to it, the most exotic looking Indian men all came in beautiful clothes and with wonderful horses. It was very interesting to see the Indian culture. The men were very aristocratic looking, with long hair, beautifully braided with ribbons or something intertwined. They had very elegant blankets or shirts and were taller and thinner than the poor women who were much squatter with broader hands and faces, and seemed to do all the work. The men in the square in Santa Fe squatted down by the walls, and seemed to spend all their days there, looking very colourful. I guess they used to be the hunters, but now there was no need to hunt, they seemed to do nothing. After it rained the poor women were mixing the adobe mud with water to make thick slurry and were patching all the walls. The rain used to wash away the adobe, as it ran off their roofs, they didn't have gutters.

Thais in Cambridge wrote to me and gave me some interesting titles of books to read, so as soon as I had any time I got Willa Cather's books—'Death comes to the Archbishop' etc. They were all written about the Santa Fe area.

The various Indian reservations in that area were so interesting, Acoma, the sky City, we climbed up to that on a really cold day in the fall, very few people were living there then, but it would have been a great place to live in the summers as it was fairly high and breezy, but the day we were there it was a tremendous icy cold wind. We visited several stone cities, Chaco Canyon, Mesa Verde, Wupatki, Canyon de Chelly. Our local Indian reservations we took trips out all the time to—Santo Domingo, Jimez, San Felipe, Tesuque, Las Truchas, Isleta, San Juan, Picuris, Chimayo, Nambe, Zune, we had never dreamed that there were so many different groups of Indians, and so many wonderful pueblos to visit.

We often went, when we heard they had a festival or some special Indian ceremony with dances, like the Shalako. We went to one, which was a rabbit dance, and they released a hare, which was dashing round and all the Indian children were trying hard to catch it. It came fairly near to us and Nils who was always very alert, jumped up quickly and caught it. I remember all the Indians looked very disapprovingly at this blonde foreign looking kid who had been so quick. Nils let it go again and then the Indian children continued their game.

Our trip to Chaco Canyon we made in the autumn of 1967, on our way up to Durango, and we stayed there a couple of nights. The children loved the very old train in Durango, and we went over to Mesa Verde from there and climbed down to see the stone houses that were built into a sort of cave in the face of the rocks. It was quite a mystery why the houses had all been abandoned, but with our 4 children I could see the dangers of living in such a high perch, maybe they left because too many people were falling off and getting killed.

Our other long trip we made, on Thanksgiving. I drove across to the Grand Canyon. We stayed in the great old Fred Harvey Lodge on the south rim It was the last weekend the Lodge was open before the winter and we thought it was freezing cold. We visited several spots along the rim. Then we went down south from Flagstaff and saw Montezuma's Castle on the way down to Phoenix. We drove out to Taliesin, which was the Western school of Frank Lloyd Wright's and we went round and saw all the studios and students work. It was a lot milder down there than at the Grand Canyon.

When we lived in Chicago in 1954, we visited many of the Frank Lloyd Wright early houses in that area, and north on the lake in Wisconsin. We really liked those, the warm wood colors in the interiors. We also took a trip to his Johnson Wax building, but that seemed to be a very illogical, what I call "stunt building", with all the glass tubing joined together with some caulking, perhaps it was experimental or just cutting edge technology. When you walked through the connections from one building to the next, these tubular windows made you feel quite dizzy. They also leaked. I had heard how many of his clients were bankrupted by his expensive rather impractical designs.

I felt the Guggenheim Museum in New York was another poor design. It has a long spiral ramp with exhibits on the walls as you walk down. There is no feeling of individual galleries, where you can group a related collection. I think the fame that the US bestowed on him, at some point, went to his head. We had met him a few times. When we saw him in Taliesin East, we went up with our architect friend from Italy—Angelo Mangiarotti and while we were talking with him, Wright's wife came in with a goose under her arm to show us, and he quickly dismissed her by telling her we had certainly not come to see her and her goose! I guess I was disappointed.

It seemed strange for me to be at home each day, just Sam and I. We got some amazing strong winds and we were fairly near the outskirts of town, so the tumbleweed would go bouncing past the house. I tried several times to clean the windows as they had a misty look to them, but I discovered that the glass had been sand blasted by the strong winds blowing sand onto the windows. On hot days in the fall we would go to some friends from the University, who had a swimming pool, and that was a wonderful way to cool your body down. Our house had an air conditioner on the roof, but it made the air feel very damp and cold, and unpleasant. It was essential though as we had a flat roof and the house without it would have been impossible. It certainly was a very difficult climate to get used to. It was very dry and so everyone's hair was hard to control, and most people who had lived there for several years seemed to have bad sinus problems from the dryness and the extremes in the climate and temperature.

We found there were some interesting people teaching at UNM, some in the English department and art department as well as architecture so we had a very pleasant social group. I was interested to see a number of faculty wives, who had had their children while they were very young, before having any career or sorting out their own lives first. Many of them were going back to school, and were often out when their children came home, so the children would come round to us or sit outside and wait. Some women did not seem content with their present lives, I thought it was so sad as it seemed to be all the wrong way round, you really shouldn't take on children until you have started a satisfying career and then after the children's needs, as they get older and you have more time, carry on with your own goals.

We were in touch with Mort and Eve Moore, who we had met on our ski holiday in 1959, in Serfaus in Austria, they were living in Los Angeles near to the UCLA campus, and asked us if we would like to visit them that Christmas. We decided to go as we knew the children had been missing our trips to the sea.

The area around Flagstaff, had had a huge amount of snow, so I decided rather than risk driving and getting caught we would take the train from Albuquerque to Los Angeles. It was a very exciting ride as the snow was so deep, they had cut a shaft for the train to go through round Flagstaff so we could only see white snow to the top of the train windows.

When we arrived in Westwood the weather was really warm and summer like, it was a wonderful change because Albuquerque had been very cold, with freezing winds. We went down to Mort and Eve's nearest beach a lot, at the end of Sunset Boulevard, and the children were delighted to be back in the ocean, we had really missed the sea living in New Mexico. The air was filled with wonderful perfumes from all the flowering plants and bushes and I think we were all won over to the Californian life.

Geoffrey went to see Charles and Ray Eames, but we both realised he had to be much nearer to them for the material he needed. When we got back to Albuquerque we set about planning to have Geoff go over to teach in California. Tim Vreeland, who was the head of the architecture school in UNM was leaving at the end of the school year and going to teach at UCLA. The nearest architecture school needing faculty was at Cal Poly in San Luis Obispo, so Geoff applied to go there.

We continued with our busy life in UNM, there were still so many areas that we wanted to visit, so on weekends and holidays we made those trips. As we got nearer to the summer we found out the temperature really heated up. I decided we should join a sports club with a lovely big outdoor pool, because it was too hot to go outside, and everyone stayed in air-conditioned buildings, but if we swam in that dry climate, the rapid evaporation cooled us off tremendously.

We had some amazing storms, you could see them swirling across the dusty desert areas, some of them would land on us, and they were very dramatic. We had one or two huge windstorms, which blew down many of the neon signs on businesses on Lomas street, we could see them from our house. We also had torrential rain storms that flooded the whole street, washing Sam's wooden tricycle away, and our garden at the back of the house, which was just bare dirt with no plants, became five or six inches deep mud. When the rain had stopped Sam and Tanya went out and were diving into the mud, they both seemed to love it, after all our dry weather it was pretty exciting.

Tim Vreeland loved to go horseback riding so most Sunday mornings he and I took the children to stables and rented some very good horses and rode along the sandy dry arroyo beds. The desert soft sandy dirt, was wonderful to gallop horses on, some of the best rides I had had in years. They had one or two English saddles, with the short stirrups but most of the saddles were Western ones with the big pummel in front and long stirrups.

Through the university we could visit D.H.Lawrence's ranch near Taos, it had been left to the University of New Mexico. It was in a very beautiful area and it still had his house, and an outdoor bee-hive oven that he had built to bake bread. Freda his wife had brought his body back from Europe and had him buried there in Taos. One of their friends Brett, was still around, we used to see her in a restaurant occasionally, she was very deaf and had one of the old fashioned ear trumpets, which seemed to work very well as she could point it at the person she was talking to, and so all the other voices in a restaurant did not confuse the sound.

The modern amplification devices amplify everything so in a group of people, it is impossible to hear what one person is saying to you. Mummy used a modern one, and said it was a babble, she found it very frustrating.

The Lawrence Ranch had some small cabins that UNM faculty could rent, they were amazingly cheap, I think only two dollars per night. We went up there in the winter when there was snow everywhere and the children thought it was great to peer out of our tiny windows and see the swirling snow. Taos and Santa Fe were quite a high altitude, Albuquerque was six thousand feet and they were much higher.

There were several communes in the area; of course this was the 60's. We had a friend Steve Baer, who was building some interesting domes and structures in the communes. I remember one large dome that was covered with triangular panels of metal, cut out of the tops of old cars. There were so many disused cars everywhere so there was no shortage of metal panels. Steve taught one class at UNM, I think on solar heating. He and his wife Holly lived in a solar house he had built for the family. The southfacing wall had metal drums, all piled in rows with insulated panels on both sides. In the daytime the outside panels were opened to allow the barrels to heat up, and the inside panels were all closed. Then at night the outer panels were closed and the inner ones opened, so that they heated the house interior, when the weather was colder.

The communes we visited seemed to have a lot of inhabitants from wealthy suburban families and they didn't seem to have any idea how to survive without their parent's care and households. They wanted to break away from the parents generation and the structure they had had as children, but didn't have any idea how to plan one of these communities to work properly. I think most of the communes, were closed down by the health authorities.

When school and university finished for the summer we started packing up our things and planning our move to California. These moves were always very tiring for me, as I had to do most of the packing and as Geoffrey never drove, I had to do all the driving too. We drove by way of the Hoover dam, which was a very impressive sight and then we went on to Las Vegas.

What a crazy place that was, in the middle of the desert! We had stopped at one or two motels on the way over and the children had gone in the swimming pools each time as it was so hot, and poor Nils got an ear infection, which was really painful when we were in Las Vegas. I asked our hotel people for the nearest doctor and Nils and I went to this very weird place in a basement. The waiting room had only old people in, and they all looked like they'd lost all their money gambling and were there because they were contemplating suicide! Very sad characters, but we did get an antibiotic for Nils there. When we went to bed in Las Vegas around 11.30 p.m. the temperature was still around 98 degrees so about 4.30am I woke everyone up and we got out on to the road, it was just flat desert from there and I thought we would fry later in our car as we didn't have air-conditioning. We came through the Mojave Desert, and then on to a wonderful road with very lush citrus trees on both sides and that led straight into Ventura. It was quite early in the morning so we went to the beach there and just lay on the sand, it was wonderful. Cool air and back to the sea again.

Our old friend Les Marzolf from our Hollywood visit in 1953, had married someone called Barbara White, and they were living on Foothill Rd., in Santa Barbara. They had a trailer for camping and had come out to visit us in New Mexico. When we left the beach in Ventura we only had to go as far as Les and Barbara's house in Santa Barbara, and we spent the night there, and the next day drove on to San Luis Obispo, where Geoff was going to teach at Cal Poly.

One of the faculty and his wife had found us a little house to rent on California Blvd. so we moved straight in there. We had to look around quickly for some furniture, beds etc., but it was amazingly easy in a University town to find things. We got some paint and redid a few of the walls to liven the house up.

It was a very good time to be teaching at Cal Poly, there was a large group of faculty from Europe and all over the world, lots of very interesting people. Several Swiss with their families, Elisabeth and Tobias Indermuhle from Berne, two brothers, the Otts from Schafhausen, Dieter and Odile Ackernecht from Zurich, and Bob and Trudi Linders from Frieborg, some Germans from Berlin, english, Ken and Jean White, Jan Lubizc-Nycz a polish Architect and Ena his wife who was from Scotland, two Egyptian professors one was called Halim Halim, 3 French architects who shared the year between them. Tom and Ann Johnson who had come from New Zealand, but Ann was originally from Norway. John and Eleanor Reur, he was from Berlin and she from N. Carolina. Robin was English and Ninou was French. He was supposedly working on a Ph.D at Stanford, which he never finished, but was teaching in the drama dept. at Cal Poly.

I remember a great theatre performance that Giles (our friend from London, who was studying Mathematics at Cuesta College) and Dieter were in, they should both of them have gone on the stage as a career, such colourful characters. Ninou, Robin's wife, was very french still, she had long auburn hair, and huge breasts, one of our barbecues on the nude beach she was cooking and swinging her big breasts all around, we were all very amused! There were a lot of interesting Americans too, one our very good friend Carleton Winslow who taught History of Architecture. He was the son of the famous Carleton Winslow who had designed many outstanding buildings in California, including the California Expostion of 1915 in San Diego, and the Los Angeles Public library in 1917. Winslow Senior, opened an office in Santa Barbara, where he designed the Santa Barbara Museum of Natural History, which is a very attractive building, he also built several houses. His son Carleton Junior was a very colorful character.

Geoffrey and Carleton taught summer school in the University in La Jolla for 2 summers. We all went down there and we stayed on the beach with our camper we had bought. Poor Carleton had a series of disaster marriages; he always picked the wrong person. He used to come around to our house for dinner and he said he would love to have a house run like ours, and before we knew what he was up to, he married an English woman who taught at Cuesta College, she had 2 children from an earlier marriage and Carleton bought them mini-bikes and all sorts of things, before he married their mother, and then the marriage lasted about a month!

Carleton's History of Architecture classes were very popular, and he had some great slides and was a very likeable character. Sandra and Jim Bagnall who came down from Berkeley, Don and Caryl Koberg, they were both from New Orleans. There were about 60 architecture professors so we had a lively social scene.

There were still a few of the old faculty from way back, George Hasslein was the head of the architecture and he was a real dud. We were still in touch with Chris Norberg Schultz in Oslo (he was our friend from Harvard in 1952) he had married an Italian architect and they had 4 children, same ages roughly as ours, Chris had visited us in Spencer House while we lived in London. He had written a very well known book on architectural education, and he was teaching in University in Oslo, and thought it would be great to join us in San Luis for a year, while he was on sabbatical. We talked to Hasslein about it, but he had never even <u>heard</u> of Chris, he must have been the only person involved in teaching architecture who would have said that, so we were not able to get Chris to join us. It would have been such a feather in Hasslein's cap.

The 60's were a strange time, the young people were suddenly ignoring all their staid parents' generation. The clothes were wild, and the music was also. 'Jesus Christ Superstar' was heard everywhere, and 'Hair' was given as a performance by the architecture students. It was very good, John Reur who was from Berlin, on the faculty joined the cast at one stage and lay across the arms of a chorus line and they were tossing him up in the air! The old faculty must have been very shocked.

Our first summer in the USA, in Albuquerque we had to pack up and travel to California and get settled for the new term, but all the succeeding summers I took the 4 children back to Europe. I wanted them to feel at home there and appreciate all the different countries. I always had work to do on Spencer House, maintenance, and if one of the four flats was changing tenants, I had to clean and often do some re-painting, and then find new tenants. It was very depressing because each time I left it, it looked wonderful, and the following summer it was all filthy again. Geoffrey stayed behind hoping to get on with his book on Charles and Ray Eames, as during the school year he didn't have any time.

Our 2nd summer in the US, I decided that after a stay in London where I had to do work on Spencer House, and find new tenants for our flat, we would go over through east Germany to see John Reur who was visiting his parents in west Berlin. My Father was horrified that I was starting out with 4 children on my own (Sam was only 4 years old) to drive in our rented car down to Dover and over the

Channel to Belgium and on into West Germany and then through the Iron Curtain into the Russian sector, because of his memories of the war. I felt once we got through to Berlin, John would help us out, as I do not speak any German.

Our first problem when we got to Dover was that our rented car could not leave England, but they assured me that they had the same model waiting in Ostend. That is a longish sail over and we were tired and when we got off the boat we found they only had a small Volkswagon bug waiting for me, and no other cars!! I was so mad, as it was far too small for 5 of us, and our luggage. The first night we drove to Brussels and stayed there, the main square with all the old painted buildings was floodlit, and was beautiful. Then we headed over into Germany, I remember Nils had an upset stomach, but the rest of us had to eat, unluckily as we were finishing, Nils threw up on the table, so we left in great haste!

We took a large autobahn headed for Berlin, it was all through the Russian sector and I remember people standing on the bridges over the freeway, watching cars from the west driving along. This was when the East and West of Germany were completely divided. People were trying to escape from the East sector by any means possible, swimming over the lake in Berlin, from the East to the West, trying to climb the walls dividing the two, and jumping off bridges on the autobahns on to the top of trucks. As we approached Berlin there were lots of road signs about different sectors, which I did not understand, and I took a left fork. The road was suddenly empty. The children all said I had gone the wrong way, but of course on a freeway you can't just turn around, and immediately these Russian soldiers came driving out to stop me. They told me how to turn around and were not too scary.

We had an exciting stay in Berlin. John's family was in the West Berlin sector, and we stayed in a hotel there near the Kurfurstendam. It was a tremendous hot spell of weather, temperatures were in the

Nineties each day and nothing seemed to be air-conditioned, as it was very unusual to have such heat. We went to Wansee, a very large lake, with John and his wife Eleanor and their two children, and swam in the lake and had Erdbeer, which was a beer with raspberries in it, and was attracting swarms of wasps! It was not a very relaxing swim because the Russians had patrol boats going back and forth down the centre of the lake, to make sure nobody tried to swim across to freedom, but at least it cooled us down.

We went over to East Berlin a couple of times. You had to go through checkpoint 'Charlie.' The soldiers took everything out of the car to examine it, luckily, we had been told by John, not to take any reading material as they would confiscate it all. They had a mirror on little wheels, and they pushed it under our car to see if we had any extra tanks welded on underneath. Apparently some people had escaped to the West by hiding in a container welded on the bottom of cars.

We had a wonderful visit to the Pergamum Museum in the East sector, where they have some amazing Egyptian exhibits; the famous head of Nefertiti is there. We drove round and looked in the shopping areas, there was really nothing for sale, it was a very sad sight and the buildings were in a bad state of repair. They had not demolished a lot of the bombed buildings, and Nils was very delighted to find lines of machine gun fire holes, across buildings. He always wanted me to tell him about the bullet strafing of the walls on the way down to the Rotherhithe tunnel in London, under the Thames. One evening in the West sector we were next to 'The Wall' and they had built wooden steps on the West side that you could climb up and look over the top. There were two walls, with a stretch of no man's land between probably 50 or 60 feet wide, and they had wooden towers erected in this no man's land, with armed soldiers in them. We climbed up at night and they had searchlights going up and down the strip of land. Lots of people that did climb over the East wall and tried to run across were shot and killed in this area. John's parents had never been allowed to visit the East of Berlin, and were telling us how difficult and depressing it was to live in the west as there was nowhere you could drive to, all you could do was fly out. The road we had driven in on, was all in the Russian sector, and was closed to Berliners. There were a lot of suicides and mental breakdowns in West Berlin.

Sarah was terribly interested in it all, she was amazed that they would have tried and succeeded to split a huge capital city into two. When we got home to San Luis Obispo, she gave a talk to the whole of the high school about her experience. She never seemed to mind addressing a large audience, a thing I have never been able to do. Think she got that from Geoff.

When we left Berlin we drove west again and went to see our old friends John and Joy Brinkworth in Holland. They had moved to Holland, and had a lovely old house in Loosedrecht, which was the place we had visited with Sarah when she was 6 months old. Joy had made their house really beautiful, she had painted murals on the walls, and had created a fantastic garden; she has such a talent for this. That was where we stayed. John was very busy with lots of commissions to paint people's portraits. He was asked to paint several members of the Royal Family. Holland was a very good place for him to live as wealthy Dutch people still thought in terms of oil paintings of themselves and their families.

We went up to Amsterdam and sailed on the canals, and we went to visit Edam and see all the cheeses in the square all being weighed. Sarah enjoyed going with Sue and Wendy, Joy's daughters, to Rotterdam and a large new shopping centre. We had to return to England, and it was soon time to fly back to the States.

San Luis Obispo was only a small town then and Cal Poly was about the only employment in town, it had a large agricultural school, and we met Vacek and Eva Cervinka from Czechoslovakia. Vacek was an engineer and teaching engineering for tractors and machinery. He and Nils were building a Go-cart in our garage. Nils used to run the engine very fast and loved the roar that it made. Vacek was worried it would be too fast, so he and Nils worked on gearing it down to a slower speed. When it was finally ready, they took it out onto our drive, and it would hardly move, it was geared down too much. Nils was very fed up, and while Eva and Vacek had dinner with us, Nils had completely dismantled it all, wanting to gear it back up!

We saw a lot of Eva as she was not involved in the school at all, so would come around for tea and go with us to the beach. She was a very entertaining person and Vacek was very sober and down to earth, they were not a good pair together and were not getting on very well. One night we were going to a party and I asked Eva to join Geoff and me, and when we were there I introduced her to a student from Argentina that I knew, he had been in some of Geoff's criticisms of student work, and was a very handsome Italian looking guy called Alberto Bertolli, from Argentina. Eva and he got on like a house on fire, and after a short time she separated from Vacek, and later married Alberto. When he finished his studies they moved to Los Angeles. He was in a big architectural office there, and they had an apartment in Westwood. Eva was the manager of the large apartment building.

We saw them a lot in those days. Eva loved practical jokes; she and her Czech friend Marta would phone and order a dinner very late at night, to be delivered to the other one, or to someone else, which of course they had to pay for, crazy things like that. When Alberto came in from work she would often hide, and one time Alberto came in and realized she was lying on the floor behind the settee, so he sat on it and pushed it back squashing her, so she had to quickly come out!

Her Czech friend, Marta, was married to Tom Gartland, and he was the manager of the Andrews Hotel in San Luis Obispo. They had an apartment in the hotel, and often on Saturday nights would have people drop in for a party. One Saturday a very English looking chap in a London business suit came, he was passing through on a tour of America, and had a friend who had been in the Peace Corps in Africa, who had known Tom there, and asked him to look him up. His name is Giles Warrack, and he was from London. We are still great friends and he is such an amusing and delightful guy. At that same party was a girl called Kay Schneider who made batiks, she lived in a little house at Avila Beach, and Giles moved in with her later. His trip around the US stopped there, he didn't continue on. After a while he took some classes at Cuesta College, and then transferred to Cal Poly, probably in 1970. He studied mathematics there. Giles and Kay later married and had one daughter, Simone. They moved to Iowa where Kay was from, and Giles finished his math degree, and taught there for a time. Then he moved on his own and left Kay, to teach in Greensboro, N. Carolina.

He is now married to Luba from Moscow, USSR. She came to the U.S. for a year, she was a scientist, and whilst she was here, she met Giles. He went over to Russia after her year was up, to the US Embassy with her to get permission for her to come back here and marry him. He has worked for 2 or 3 summers for the navy in San Diego so we have been able to see them then, and Geoff and I went to stay with them in Greensboro. *(An update on Giles and Luba, they have twice visited us in Santa Barbara. Luba is making beautiful jewelry, of silver and semi-precious stones, so I asked a group of our friends to come in, and they bought some of her beautiful ear rings, necklaces etc. They have just been here staying—August 2005—and came with Luba's daughter Jane from Russia and her husband who are living in San Francisco.)*

As Sam was only little I took him a lot to Avila beach, which was always a very sociable spot. Various Cal. Poly wives went there with their children, Elisabeth Indermuhle had 2 little boys, and Eleanor Reur had a boy, a little older than Sam. There was an English girl called Jeanine who was married to Charles Cahill, he was the life guard at Avila, a big handsome surfer guy, and they had a little boy too.

One of the first things I did was buy myself a surf board, in those days they were still the big boards, and for me they were much more stable than the smaller boards. The advantage of the small boards is that they are much more maneuverable, and can be taken up and down on the face of a wave, so surfing really changed when they were introduced. There were often nice waves by the pier in Avila so I usually had my board there, and left it at the Cahill's. Geoff was teaching the 5th year students in 'Z' lab, with Don Koberg, and some of the guys were really a wild bunch, they had been studying architecture for many years, having to repeat several incomplete terms. They all seemed to drink heavily, and maybe smoked pot, were from wealthy families who had allowed them to be quite undisciplined. They were a very attractive gang though, but had got the '60's bug. Anyway they were often sitting on their boards with me waiting to catch a wave. I asked them why they weren't at some interesting lecture, that I knew Geoff had organised, but they said what had I done when I was young that was so great, and I had to admit that I had always taken life very seriously, and never had a time until then that I could relax and goof off. I was already forty five, and had been hard at studies and work all those years, I wondered if I had got it the wrong way round? Even starting surfing so late I really loved it, the silent power of a big wave behind your shoulder, pushing you in front of it. I found it was terribly exciting.

I surfed pretty much all the time we were in San Luis, Nils got into it fairly early on and he had a pal at school, David Asher who was a very keen surfer too, so I used to drive them out to Pismo Beach as they loved the waves there and when they had the day free on weekends I would leave them there for the whole day. I had one or two really painful wipe-outs, and nearly bust my front teeth, so I gradually had to drop out from that sport.

I joined a good tennis group at Cuesta College and played there a lot; I had played a lot of tennis in New Mexico too. I also joined an archaeology class at Cuesta College, they were going to various American Indian sites in the area, looking for rock paintings and skulls and artifacts. I think Georgia Fleishman was the one who got me into it. She followed it up by studying with Skip Cole at UCSB, and is now quite an expert. She spent years on Easter Island and has written several books and done programmes on TV.

The children still enjoyed horse riding so I used to go with them. One Sunday we had some friends visiting who wanted to ride with us, so we were quite a crowd, and the stables said they were one horse short, so I said I would wait and catch them up. They soon saddled up a really wild animal, and brought him out, and I took off, we were riding in Pismo, and had to cross the railway line to get to the beach. The stubborn animal refused to go over the tracks, and I was determined to go over, it was rearing and backing up, and finally threw me off. I grabbed the reins and dragged it across the tracks, and we caught up with the others. I remember my hands were cut from the very sharp edge of the pummel on my saddle, I think I had grabbed at it on my way down!

The faculty was all terribly friendly and we had lots of potluck parties and dinners and cookouts on the beach. The Otts (two brothers) from Switzerland, had rented a small house on Pismo Beach, right on the sand, so we would go down and dig up some clams in front of their door and then cook them for our dinner. The other beach parties were at Montana de Oro, where the mussels were very good, we got a fire going and cooked them straight away with white wine and some garlic. It was a terribly sociable time there; I don't know how it happened because it is not like that any more.

Jack and Sheri Augsburger had Jack's studio out at Shell Beach, where he made banners and all sorts of iron objects. He was not on the faculty but a lot of us knew him, and that was also a very popular place to hang out. Jack and Sheri had a crowd of children, I think about 8. Jack was a very interesting macho sort of guy, and would have long discussions around the fire. Unfortunately he had heart trouble and I guess did not take his medication, so he died when he was in his Forties, which was a terrible shock to everyone.

Our old friend Les Marzolf was still living in Santa Barbara, and we visited him quite often. He had a Jeep and a trailer and he wanted us to borrow it, and take a trip to Mexico that following Christmas, 1968. Tom (in the art department) and Ann Johnson had 3 children, Sarah, Nils and Tanya's ages, so we decided to go down together. The Johnsons had a tent, and we stopped at Les' house and got the Jeep and camper there and then I started to drive down to Baja. I had never pulled any trailer, and it was very difficult when I got onto a dead end street in San Diego, to try to turn it round!

We had a good holiday and the children enjoyed all the fireworks on Christmas Eve. We went down to Ensenada, and did some fishing and looking at different places. We had one huge wind—storm, and the Johnson's tent blew down in the middle of the night, so they had to find a motel. On the way home I almost lost the trailer, it just started swinging from side to side, and the Jeep had a very short wheel-base so it was swinging us all around too. Luckily there were no cars near us, or we should have had a terrible accident.

The whole camping idea seemed to work well though, as there were six of us, motels and eating out in restaurants all the time would have been too expensive, but it would have been easier for me. After driving all day with the trailer, I had to make up beds and do the cooking, but I really enjoyed all the trips we made. It did give us the possibility to go and see most of the places that we had heard about and would not otherwise have visited, so I went ahead and bought a camping vehicle of our own.

When the children had a long weekend from school, I used to take them down to Refugio Beach, near Santa Barbara, a wonderful horseshoe shaped sandy beach with a row of huge palm trees. This is the same beach my grown children are now enjoying the ocean with their kids. We spent the days swimming and the boys surfing, and we went into Santa Barbara a few times to shop and look around. It seemed a lovely European sort of town. Sarah's friends from high school had cars and would come down and join us, and Nils friend, Gretchen Augsburger and Tanya's friend Kirsty Johnson came with us too. Once you get into the slow pace of doing nothing much, a holiday like that is very relaxing.

The next Christmas, in 1969, we drove over to Tucson where our friends Mort and Eve Moore (who we first met in 1959 originally skiing in Serfaus Austria,) were spending Mort's sabbatical year. We saw some lovely old mission churches and had a day in Old Tucson, which was like a film set of all the typical Wild West scenes, they even had actors doing a performance of a big chase, and bandits and shooting. There were a lot of old Indians sitting on benches, they were just dummies, but the children sat next to them for their photos. We traveled on down into Mexico to Nogales and had Christmas Day down there in our camper. I think the children enjoyed it all and as we didn't have any family in the States, it was a great way to spend the holiday.

For the Easter break that year 1970 we went to Death Valley with our Swiss friends, Tobias and Elizabeth Indermuhle. They were from Berne and had come over for a year, Tobias was teaching architecture at Cal Poly. They had two little boys Lawrence and Jon. For people from Switzerland and England, Death Valley is quite amazing. Zabriski Point where they made the film, and all the canyon areas that seemed like they had been sculpted by water, but I don't know where or when the water came from. We camped next to each other in a vast sandy desert area, in the daytime it was very hot, but at the same time we could see the snow peaks around Mount Whitney, the highest mountain in the United States.

For that year 1969 to 70 we were living in a house on Hope Avenue that belonged to some friends of ours the Millers. He was a school psychologist and he had a sabbatical, so they took their children and went to Wales for the year. As it was a bigger house than our last one, we asked my parents to come over to stay. They had a few places they wanted to see so Sam and I took them over to Yosemite and to see the Giant Redwoods. Poor Daddy was very worried by the heat as we drove through the Valley. My Barracuda car did not have air-conditioning and as we went through miles and miles of barren sandy areas Daddy kept saying it was a 'desperate' place to be! They loved Yosemite though, and all the cooler areas.

From San Luis Obispo I took them to see the Big Sur coast and the various missions San Miguel and San Antonio. We were pleased that they had felt so adventurous to come over, as we had wanted them to come ever since our first stay in the US in the early 50's. They had booked their return flight from San Francisco as they really wanted to pay a visit there, so we all drove up and stayed in a nice hotel with them, and took them to see the different interesting spots, and then we had to take them to the airport and say goodbye.

As the plane was touching down in Los Angeles, they were not allowed to buy any duty-free in San Francisco. Mummy decided to get off the plane in Los Angeles and went to buy Daddy some drinks and cigarettes from Duty Free. She went back to the plane she had just left, she thought, and when she got on it, looked around for Daddy and everybody was Japanese! It was a terrible shock for her, but she was able to get help to get back to the plane where Daddy was waiting! (He was 68 then, and still very lame, so it was very adventurous for them to come over)

As the Millers were coming home that summer from Europe and we were tired of moving around, we decided to buy a house on Spring Court. We suddenly felt much more settled as we had had three years in different rented places. We did quite a few things to the House, opened up some walls, and painted it too. Nils did a conversion in the garage for himself and his drums, which were very noisy. While we were there I did a very pleasant new garden at the back of the house, as it had been very dismal.

Nils found a motorbike that had been abandoned on the campus, so he brought it home and worked on it and got it running very well. He had a friend Dan Roguaway who had one too, so they used to go riding up the railroad tracks on Cuesta Grade, and all round. I'm not sure how we managed to get the motorbike out to the beach, but I have some photos of Sam on the back of Nils' bike, riding along on Pismo Beach.

That Easter 1971 we took our camper and went up to San Francisco, we had some very good friends there, Barbara Bramson and her husband. They were English, Bram had worked in England, on the jet engine invention with Whittle, and while he had been in the States he had invented the heart and lung machine, which made it possible to carry out surgery on the heart and lungs while his machine took over their job. They had been friends of Peter and Lois Day, our good friends from Blackheath, when they had been living in San Francisco, and Lois asked us to go and see them. They had not had any children but really enjoyed ours. After paying them a visit we went to the Sacramento River basin, and followed a small road on the south side of the river, there were some beautiful old mansions on the riverbanks, and I remember there was an eerie mist hanging over the water each evening. We went up to Sacramento, and then up to Placerville, where we took the 49er route south through all the old gold rush towns. I remember Angel's Camp and Columbia were very beautiful old places, and they still had some beautiful old buildings, old bars with double swinging half doors and old shops, and a theatre. It was good to see some old things that had been preserved for a change.

We swung around to go to Badger's Pass, where they still had quite a lot of snow, so we rented some skis for Nils and Tanya, Sam was very happy just playing in the snow. Nils in his typical wild fashion took off down a slope with a big bump in it, so he really did a big ski-jump on his first time on skis! It was a lovely Easter break from the children's school and Geoff's teaching. When we got back home we left Geoff and went down to Refugio Beach near Santa Barbara for a few days. Sam and Tanya caught some sweet baby rabbits. Those two were always very keen on animals. Once we had our own house they each had a cat, Tigger and Bomb. We had chinchillas and hamsters and Tanya had a rat and guinea pigs. I have a photo of Sam while we were at Refugio with a snake around his neck! Sarah and Nils' friends came down and brought their tent to stay next to us, so there were a lot of folk to feed. I think that was the time that Ena Lubicz Nycz from Scotland, came down with us too, and brought the first of our cheesecakes, and gave me her recipe.

More troubles in Spencer House

In April I heard from the tenants in the lowest floor of Spencer House, in London, that they had giant 'mushrooms' growing inside on the party wall. I knew it was our dreaded dry rot. In May I flew over there to sort it all out. It had gone through 4 floors, from the very top of the house the box gutter, to the bottom, but luckily it had stayed near the party wall. Our neighbour, who was the wrecker of old buildings, had a broken rain water pipe which had been spraying water on that part of the wall, all the winter. Dry rot is a plant, growing on timber and can only grow with moisture, but of course it destroys any wood it meets, so we had a huge problem. When I was living there I used to go out with an umbrella when it rained and check my box gutters and down pipes were handling all the water.

I got in a big firm of contractors because it was a very large job, they had to take out the lintels on all 4 floors and replace them with concrete and cut the ends off all the floor joists and the ceiling joists, take down all the wood lath ceilings and go at least five feet beyond any infected parts. They treated the brickwork too, to try to kill all the spores, which cause the outbreaks. Our old cat Shusha from the days we lived there, was still alive and being fed by the people in our flat. The whole trip was very depressing, I went to see the Department of the Environment responsible for historic buildings, but of course there was nothing they could do, no funds available, and they were a pathetic feeble group. They wrote to Nightingale once again but got no further than before. Dry rot in England is a real nightmare as it spreads so fast.

Sarah had been saving all her babysitting money, and she and her great friend Donna Asher had tickets to go to Europe for the summer. Jean, Donna's Mother and I took them up to San Francisco to get their flight. We were sitting in the restaurant at the airport worrying if they would manage without us, and they announced over the loud speakers that they had found Donna's purse with money, passport and tickets etc. Jean and I couldn't believe it! However they did have a great summer over there, staying with my parents and a lot of our friends, they travelled all over. My Aunt Joan had a friend who was married to a Doctor in Beaune, France, and as Sarah was so good at languages she decided to go and stay with this family to use her French in conversation.

Poor lass had a miserable time with them, she was still young, only 15, and like a lot of California kids at that time, she loved wandering around with bare feet, and she also never wore a bra, so the family were very upset! They had 2 sons and a daughter. One night there had been a film on TV about one of the wars, poor Sarah didn't know all the details of European history, but when they all sat down to eat they were all attacking her about the way the British had behaved towards the French, I think Sarah was almost in tears. If I had been there I would have reminded them about France's errors as allies, and had their whole family crying! How France constructed the Maginot Line, at a tremendous cost in World War II. The supposed impregnable border, against the Germans, was overtaken in a matter of hours. British troops were caught and stranded. Many died and were captured, when without any warning France quickly surrendered. When I had these discussions with my French fiancé, Pierre (see my 1st book), he would put his head in his handkerchief and cry.

When I got back to SLO we decided not to go to Europe that summer as I had only just returned from the dry rot troubles, and Sarah and Donna were over there. We thought we would take a trip to Canada. My Barracuda which had been such a great car for us was now four years old and my mechanic thought I should get a bigger car to pull the camper all that way, so I went and bought a new Ford station wagon for the trip.

We started up on 101 going north and we were just past Paso Robles (30 miles) when my brakes went out, and the passenger side back wheel was on fire. Luckily I had the trailer hitched to the car, so I was able to pull the brake of the trailer and that saved us from going off the road. The children were very upset, I got the car towed to the nearest garage, and they could not find anything wrong with the brakes (they had started the fire) so we had to find a place to stay while they worked on the car. Next day we started out again, and we kept stopping to check that wheel and after a short time it was again very hot, so we got another garage to release the brakes. We had to stop at a garage every 100 or 150 miles for the whole trip. I was so fed up and really wished I had kept my Barracuda, we seemed to have got a real Ford lemon.

We went up through Napa Valley and visited several of the Vineyards, one or two had lovely buildings and we tasted some great wines. I think it was in Napa that the children were so tired of Geoff's slow shaving every morning, with his electric razor. I think he liked the massage it gave him, and took him ages, so we were all sitting waiting to get going. They decided to hide his razor, so he had to let his beard grow—and has had it ever since!

We headed on up towards Portland, and there we visited Thais Carter's son, she was our old friend in Cambridge, Mass, that we had stayed with when we first flew into Boston, on our way to Albquerque. Her son was in one of the huge timber mills, and he took us around that. We went on up to Seattle, and we had really rainy weather, so we couldn't see the snow on Mt. Rainier, or even see the mountain. We were staying in a campground with our trailer, but it was so wet and muddy so I took the family over to the restrooms in the car! Not what you would expect for midsummer.

From Seattle we put the car and trailer on a ferry over to Victoria, which the children thought was great. There was a large park called Butchart Gardens, which reminded me a lot of Happy Valley Gardens in Llandudno, Wales, and it had the same sort of evening entertainment, Scottish bagpipes included. After one or two days there we took the ferry over to Vancouver and again we really enjoyed that town, a very interesting ethnic mix of people, and a very picturesque setting for a city. We went down to see the new University, which was just built, and then we went up on the aerial tramway to the top of the mountain overlooking the town.

On our way down south we stayed in Seattle with a sweet girl who we knew from San Luis Obispo, she had been a girl friend of Rainer Ott, one of the Swiss lecturers who were with us when Geoff taught at Cal Poly. She was from the Seattle area and so she knew it well, and she showed us around, we went to a big firework display in the Exhibition area, and rode the monorail. On our last morning as we were just packing up to go south there was a sudden break in the clouds and we saw Mt Rainier for the first time, looking really fabulous! No more vivid memories from the trip, stopping all the way every 100 or so miles to get the back brakes released was one of my main thoughts, and then just south of San Francisco finding the first mechanic who really thought about and solved our problem. He carefully measured the brake disc and we had a wheel drum that was not round but slightly oval, so that the brakes automatically adjusted to one side but were too tight when the wheel rotated, causing it to over heat. We contacted Ford once again and when we were back home we got a new wheel drum, which corrected it. I had bought the brand new car to make the driving easier, as the driver it ruined my whole trip!

Up to now I have not needed to discuss my views on politics. However, one cannot come from England to the USA without noticing many differences in how the government seems to work. These are my honest views, and in good conscience I want to share them. If they distress you, dear reader, I ask you to skip forward to the next section!

On re-editing this in 2004, I have much more severe criticisms of the US!! We have just had four years of President George W. Bush. He says he has not had advice from his father, who was president before Clinton, but from his higher father (GOD!!). In my opinion, if he has been getting divine advice, he has simply not been listening to it. He got us into an unjustified war in Iraq, which has practically bankrupted our country, with TRILLIONS of dollars of debt.

Our economy is absolutely shot at the moment. Huge numbers of people have lost their jobs to 'Outsourcing', and all the big inter-net companies in the Silicon Valley have collapsed. The employees in the US want to get in on the BIG CASH GAINS that all the executives help themselves to, and call bonuses. (I thought those were given for a job well done!) With the result that many jobs have gone abroad. India and China have a far better educated work force, who will work for pennies an hour, undercutting our labour by 80% or more. I just spoke to an employee in MBNA Bank, and she had a strange accent, didn't sound Mexican, so I asked her where she was, and she told me the name of a very small town in India!

The majority of workers in the US are so badly educated, and it seems more and more difficult to find anyone, other than some industrious Mexicans, who can do an efficient days work. I am very pleased that my father is not alive still, as this situation would kill him, for sure, even I am agreeing with the 60's play "Stop the World, I Want to get OFF".

Unfortunately, poor decisions and undue influence are not limited to the national level. Even in local government we have seen what appear to be instances of improper influence, leading to building permits, which are awarded only to friends of those in power.

An example, which is especially tragic for our future generations, is the case of Val Verde. The third, and most disgraceful of our

Supervisor's acts, was in connection with Val Verde. The owner Dr. Warren Austin, had always made tours available during his 50 years of ownership. The landscaping by Lockwood de Forest is very well known, and visited by international landscape architects. Dr. Austin saw the fate of many of the big estates that were being sold and then broken up and developed, he planned very carefully to preserve his seventeen and a half acres for posterity, and making it available for tours, for everyone to enjoy. To achieve this he first had to obtain a conditional use permit (CUP) I tried to help him with his plan.

Dr. Austin invested years of effort and much money in advancing his proposal to the Planning Commission and the Board of Supervisors. He had to pay for costly traffic studies and an environmental impact report, but finally in the end his application was denied.

The future generations of Montecito, Santa Barbara, and the whole of the USA have been denied the gift that Dr. Austin tried to leave to them for their enjoyment. In the meantime Dr. Austin passed away, after a seven year, costly battle with the Authorities.

I cannot understand how Americans allow what appears to be improper influence at all levels of government, driven by unlimited politicial contributions. Coming here from a country where we have a Parliamentary System of Government it is difficult to live here where they brag about a Democracy, when we don't have one. The President is not even voted for by the MAJORITY of the people.

The latest Val Verde news in 2010 is that, the two people who Dr. Austin entrusted his precious Val Verde Estate, took out a large loan (I do not understand why the loan was taken, or where the proceeds were used) Val Verde had to declare Bankruptcy. The house was put on the market, and has been sold to a wealthy foreign Banker who moved into Montecito and has bought several large expensive houses in the area.

I realise that several main threads of my life have got lost in the account of the year, to year events of a big family, growing bigger all the time.

The steel works, which I think are such a powerful link between my great, great grandparents and me. Steel was for years our families' lifeblood and even after I had left Sheffield, I remember the wonderful smell of so much industry around, when I got off the train at the LMS station. Daddy told me when I was young 'where there's muck there's money' and it was certainly a very dirty, black foggy town. I think the hard productive work in industry has always been something I admired, and felt it was the real strength of our country.

My father for his whole life had had to watch every penny, as his income from the struggling steel works, especially during the depression, was so small and he had so many people to support, his Mother, his two sisters Dorothy and Joan, my mother, and David and me. I think that may have been the reason that when I went to University, he was very emphatic that I should have a good career and be able to support my family. That was an amazing change for someone who had been brought up with the idea that the women stayed at home, doing a little embroidery, playing the piano and running the servants in the home.

I have some small note books about two inches by three inches, that daddy kept in his pocket and entered every thing he spent, even down to a penny for his bus fare. Every evening he would empty his trouser pockets and sort out all his change, and make sure it tallied with his little book. His theory was if you watch your pennies the pounds will take care of themselves. (Getty, one of the world's wealthiest men, was of the same opinion; Getty even had pay phones installed in his house, as guests used to take advantage of his wealth and run up huge phone bills for him) My Father had a slow ritual getting ready for bed. After his trouser pockets were emptied, he would brush his trousers and put them in a trouser press. He always wore some stretch spiral bands on his arms, that were to raise his shirtsleeves, and those were taken off. He used to wear spats in the earlier days but I do not remember those. I remember the light grey ones that people wore for weddings. What a change to the new informal clothes, especially in California.

Can you imagine how hard it was for him to accept the new consumer society? Daddy always vowed he would never buy anything German. After several years Daddy decided to retire. Since his paralyzing injection he had always been very lame and it must have exhausted him to go down to the works each day.

England had a very bad period after the war to get back on its feet. All our cities were badly bombed, and the people were very short of energy, I think through our tough times and years of hardship, bombing, and very little, poor food. There was a general feeling that somebody from somewhere should repay us for our tremendous fight, for so many years all alone, until nearly the end of the war, when we got help from the USA fighting against German tyranny. We had saved the whole of Europe, alone.

Unfortunately the politicians decided that Germany needed to get back on its feet, because people said after the First World War, Germany was left leaderless and defeated, and that was how Hitler had been able to take over during the terrible depression. I remember our industrialists went over to Germany after the War to help them start up the car and steel industries. My own feeling was that we should have received that help as we were not the aggressors and for three or four years on our own we had battled the monster that Hitler had created. Daddy I know shared the same feelings.

Once we lived in America, I bought a German Volkswagen camper to keep in England, so we could spend the summer's traveling around Europe. I think it was very difficult for Daddy to see the rise of Germany and all its products flooding our markets. He hated them with a passion, having gone through two wars with them. He had only bought British goods and always Rover cars.

The steel trade was a very tough business. I remember going down to see the huge hammers, worked from an overhead gantry, each man had a furnace hearth next to him, which he kept red hot by pushing a pedal to the side with his knee, to the right, pumping air through the red coke fire, and in the coals he kept the steel blanks that he would be working on. When they were almost white hot, he pulled one out with huge tongues and started up his giant hammer to shape the bar for a large industrial file. They had brine tanks next to them and when the bars had been under the huge hammers, to shape them, they immersed them in the cold salt bath, I think this was all part of the hardening process, and there would be great hissing clouds of steam. I adored it when I was small and Daddy took me to the works. The roar of those furnaces and the crashing of a room full of giant hammers at work were very incredible, like a scene from Hades. Daddy was so proud of the files they produced, he said they would never wear out, as the guys working the hammers made the centre of the files, that get most of the wear, a deeper cut.

My brother David joined Henry Whitham in 1954, the year Pauline and he were married, after qualifying as a metallurgist and working at two steel plants in Sheffield. It was clear then that the falling demand for files, 90% of Henry Whitham sales, would eventually close the company. Many of the workmen were sons and grandsons from my great grandfather's time. In 1954 there was a serious international shortage of alloy steels and Henry Whitham was asked by one engineer, Molins Machine Co to use their influence in Sheffield to acquire one particular grade of steel for them. From this base he was able to develop this quality of steel with engineers throughout England. The demand for larger diameters increased dramatically leading to a space shortage and the purchase of a large warehouse at Carbrook Street.

Alongside this development David received enquiries and orders for large thick walled nickel alloy steel tubes for transatlantic telephone cables. The profits from this enabled him to cease file manufacture in 1966 and develop the alloy steel business. At Carbrook St they found they were short of thermal treatment capacity (All alloy steels require thermal treatment before going into service) and also for machine shop capacity, since a large quantity of orders called for initial rough machining. As a result they installed furnaces giving them a capacity of up to 2000 tonnes per week! David bought Millhouses Engineering Co. and developed and invested in that plant.

David then moved into American Steels, the AISI grades related to wellhead use for the oil industry and this required stocking bar to 1300mm dia. (8ft weighs 30 tons) and the lift capacity, sawing capacity and machine capacity had to be increased to match. Quality was and is key to the market and David's Quality Control Team was internationally respected.

Diploma purchased a controlling interest in 1970. David remained as joint shareholder and Managing Director until he retired in 1991. He says there was much less pressure on him . . . . But a job that gave much excitement and satisfaction.

I am very pleased I asked him exactly what he had done when he took over from Daddy, as I never knew all the details myself, and he and Pauline bought a beautiful property near Pezenas in the south west of France, and as I live in California I have never had a chance to get all the details before!

Now back to pick up the story of life in San Luis Obispo. Once Sammy was attending kindergarten the children were all busy in school, I made contact with Ned Roguaway, who was the Head of the San Luis Obispo County Planning Dept. He was a very interesting person, and I had met him earlier as he had been doing some teaching in the architecture department at Cal. Poly. As I had been in the Chicago Planning Commission office years before, I felt I had some ideas that would be useful still. Ned told me the office had no architects, only geographers and some planners, but he said when the power station for Morro Bay, our beautiful local fishing harbor, had come in to apply for permits. They submitted only plans with no elevations, so he had had no idea that the power plant chimneys would be so colossal, dominating the whole of Morro Bay.

I felt if I had been there I would have requested the elevations be submitted too. Ned was nervous to take me on at first, as he said the supervisors gave him very limited powers, but he added that he was worried about the developers who were pushing to develop Atascadero, another wonderful near by town, at that time.

He showed me some drawings of the scheme that had been submitted for a shopping center, which I could see was going to ruin the classical municipal building with its very old cedars of Lebanon, in front. It is a very famous landmark, and can be admired from the freeway as you drive north. I think that was why Ned asked me to work with him, Atascadero was my first job.

The developers had the most hideous design; they said if you had a Cornet Drugstore as your anchor, then other stores would follow. Cornet had a concrete block wall on three sides, and a very ugly glass wall on the entrance side. It was to be surrounded by acres of tarmac for car parking. I asked the developers if they had done any study to find out if Atascadero needed more shopping. I also made it clear that their scheme completely ruined the interesting classical setting, and they were planning to remove the beautiful, very old Cedars.

When I drew up a scheme for a possible shopping center, which would have fitted into the site in a compatible way, they said they couldn't spend much money on it, as the town didn't warrant it! Not much business and a poor district. I was pleased for a while to be able to stop them—I heard from Ned that they had gone direct to the supervisors to complain about not getting their own way. I am afraid that this type of developer ruined a lot of wonderful old small towns. We had another wretched man coming to the office, who was continually trying to get permission to quarry one of the wonderful rock formations, from one of the old volcanoes on the road out to Morro Bay. I knew that these rocks had great Indian rock art, from my archaeology classes at Cuesta College.

I heard from older staff in the planning office that the same man was continually coming back with the same plan, and that they thought he would eventually get the Supervisors majority of votes, probably when the Board members changed in his favour.

I hadn't realized the planners have no power in the USA, they are just advisors, the final decision is by the Supervisors, and the decision of these elected Officials can be influenced by special interest groups or individuals.

I had run into this disastrous type of Government in the US before, back in 1954 in Chicago. The election of all Government Officials, even at the Presidential level, involves huge cash contributions by individuals or groups, used to help the candidates get elected. When elected the officials then have a debt to the contributors.

How can old buildings and picturesque villages and natural beauty be protected from such philistines with this kind of election system, also what kind of effect is this kind of system going to have on the Country as a whole?

In England, City Planners are taken very seriously, so the profession attracts very good, high-qualified people. Their decisions are final.

I had thought that was the roll I had taken on and I was really disappointed.

After four years in San Louis Obispo, Geoffrey wanted to continue to write his book (since the beginning of our move to America.) He had very little time while he was teaching, so we decided to move south to Santa Barbara. Geoffrey would have preferred to be in Los Angeles, so he would be near Charles and Ray Eames as his book was about their work. We went down and looked in a few areas, but I heard that the schools had a big drug problem. With four children it would have been too dangerous.

Santa Barbara is the ideal size, and is a really beautiful unspoiled town. We had several friends there that we had visited and the town right on the coast, with wonderful architecture and a dramatic range of mountains as a backdrop along the oceanfront, is a perfect setting. I wished Ned luck and resigned.

Geoff or I could perhaps get an interesting job, as Santa Barbara is very appreciative of good architecture. With four young children we needed to continue working but Geoff was dedicated to his book instead! If and when it was finished, was it going to make some income?

We were able to sell our house on Spring Court in San Luis and move to a house we rented on Cima Linda Lane, in Montecito. Various friends helped us make the move and we seemed to settle fairly quickly into a new town. Nils and Tanya were at the Junior High School, downtown. Sarah was in the High School, and Sam was at a nearby school, Cleveland.

I think Sarah had a hard time with the change of town, and school. She was in her last year at the High School, and of course most of the students at that stage had their own bunch of friends. The school has quite a large number of Mexican boys, which she was not used to. She had long very blonde hair, and they used to tease her as she walked down the halls—nipping her bottom. I think she did have a couple of girls she knew, but her good friends from San Luis Obispo, especially Danny Eister, used to come down and stay with her, he had finished school in San Luis Obispo so was free to visit us frequently.

Both Sarah and Tanya got some babysitting jobs from various people we knew at the Center for Democratic Studies. We all went to the beaches (except Geoff), as they are so near, compared with the drive we had in San Luis Obispo. Nils soon had a group of friends who surfed all the time, so he was able to continue with his surfing. One of his broken boards, he reshaped and made it into a small board for Sammy, he was only seven, but soon found a great pal, Jason Gittens, who also wanted to take up surfing. I cut one of Nils' old wetsuits up and reduced its size to fit Sam. No one was making surfing gear for small children at that time, but Sammy and Jason were very keen, and soon were able to take small waves at Leadbetter Beach, and near the Biltmore pier. They have both remained avid surfers.

We had had 2 very good friends in Santa Barbara whilst we still lived in San Luis Obispo, David and Pat Gebhard. They were very welcoming and asked us to many dinners at their house, to meet people they knew we would enjoy. David was at UCSB in the History of Architecture Dept. and his wife was in the library at UCSB.

They invited one of their close friends, Hattie Von Breton once to meet us, and we both found her very interesting and very lively. She was a good friend of Charles and Ray Eames, Geoff was writing about them in his book, and Hattie had a lot of stories about them and their work. We were now near enough to LA for Geoff to make trips down there to see the Eames. He could easily take the bus down.

Hattie had a huge group of friends too; she was on the Board of the Santa Barbara Art museum, as well as the Lobero Theatre. Through her we met another group of interesting people.

Hattie was born in Porterville, California, into the Carr family, over in the valley, north of Bakersfield. We were always amazed that such a very interesting woman had come out of such a small town. Her father and one of her brothers were both doctors, and Hattie had studied Art, and had moved to Los Angeles. She had worked for Disney, and was one of their good friends. She had married Hal Von Breton, who I think was importing very fine woods from South America.

Hattie's grandfather with a group of Carr relatives had started a wonderful group of houses up in the Western Sierras. When Hattie was small all the family would go up to their cabin in the summer in horse drawn wagons. It is called Doyles Springs.

The old cabin had been burnt down, so Hattie and Hal had replaced it with a very beautiful large Scandinavian style cabin, built with some of his imported wood. As soon as we met Hattie she asked us all to go up to stay, and she asked David and Pat Gebhard to go at the same time. Everyone took food for one or two meals, and we all shared the work. We had so many happy times there. Sammy was 7 (1972) when we first went, and now (2011) we all still go, with all our grandchildren, who love it just as much as our own children did. It is such a wonderful relaxing place to visit. It is right on the river, with many waterfalls near the house, so all the rooms have a wonderful sound of tumbling water.

There is a large pool for swimming, and 2 tennis courts. Sammy soon got into the fly-fishing up there and really enjoys catching trout for breakfast, now he's teaching the grandchildren.

A few years ago Hattie died, she had made the mistake of moving out of Santa Barbara to Picayune, a small place near New Orleans, because her daughter Robin had married an attorney in New Orleans, and Robin had 2 boys, so Hattie wanted to be near them. Robin's marriage broke up soon afterwards and she moved to Arizona, to teach. Hattie was left in Louisiana on her own. She was always saying were there any reasonable price houses in Santa Barbara to move back to, but it is a very difficult town to ever return to, if you have sold your house. It is in such demand and the prices just go up and up.

Hattie got breast cancer, and had the surgery, and then she started having some health problems, so her daughters Robin and Sally moved her to a home there in Picayune, but all her family, brothers and nieces and all her friends were in California. Geoffrey and I went out to stay with her and we sailed up the Mississippi on one of the big paddle steamers, and visited some of the wonderful old mansions on the banks of the river with her. We had great fun. We really enjoyed that area, but New Orleans wasn't so good it seemed run down when we were there.

Robin and Sally, were worried about Hattie, as she had two bad falls, and was on her own, so they moved her back to California, to a nursing home north of Mill Valley, where she had many Carr relatives. Geoffrey and I visited her again there, and later Nils went up with his new baby, Dane. Hattie died soon after we had seen her.

Because the 2 daughters are not used to looking after buildings, Nils volunteered to keep his eye on things up at Doyles Springs, in the Sierras, and has done a lot of work up there. We try to go up once a year with some of our family, which now with 9 grandchildren is quite a crowd, 18 in all!

Through the University we met some interesting people. Geoff taught a few lectures in the College of Creative Studies out on the UCSB campus. I used to take him to downtown, and he would take one of the UCSB buses, as it is about 15 miles west of Santa Barbara.

One of his star pupils from New Mexico teaching days, Tommy Torres, had followed his architecture schooling with a course in Business in Berkeley, and after that had moved down to Los Angeles, to practice architecture. He invited Geoffrey down to Malibu, where he was then living, to help him work on some of his residential commissions. Geoff collaborated well on the designs with Tommy.

When our first year in Santa Barbara was over, we thought it would be good to have a stay back in London. I wanted to do some work on our old flat in Spencer House, and as the people who were renting it were leaving, it seemed a good time for us all to go over. Sarah had finished her last year of school and decided she would love to move over to Europe. We were still in touch with Ingerlise, our last au pair girl, who came from Copenhagen, and Sarah knew her very well. She decided to go to Denmark as an au pair, and found a family in a suburb of Copenhagen where she could stay, and work as an au pair.

Before she went off we took the whole family over to France with our VW camper, we also had a tent to pitch, if the weather was good. I drove down thru France and over into Italy, we went to Vicenza and Verona which have some beautiful old buildings, and then headed east to Venice. I had not been before, but Geoff had. I remember the weather was very sticky hot, and there was no place to sit down in all of Venice, so unless you went to a restaurant or bar you just had to keep walking. To keep stopping for drinks, with 6 people would have been very expensive. We were camping fairly near to the water, and the mosquitoes were very bad. I remember waking up with Sam's thin little legs hanging down from the top bunk—and he was counting all his bites, 67, 68 etc!, poor little guy.

We drove over the St. Gothard Pass and up into Switzerland, which the children seemed to like better, as they thought it all looked lovely and clean. I guess that is one thing you can say about it, but we had always been told it was the land of 'cuckoo clocks' and was very dull. We drove down into Berne to visit our Swiss friends we knew in San Luis Obispo, Tobias and Elisabeth Indermuhle. They had not been back long, so Tobias had to do his military service, which everyone in Switzerland has to do. We enjoyed Berne, it has some lovely old buildings, and their 2 boys Lorenz and Jan had fun with Nils, Tanya and Sam.

We then drove on up to Holland and stayed with John and Joy Brinkworth near Hilversum, in Loosedrecht and took the children to see Amsterdam and the windmill areas, then headed back over the channel to London. (The advantage of our VW camper, was that we could visit friends, but did not require any beds, as we could sleep in it.)

Sarah had to leave fairly soon for Denmark on her own, to start her new au pair job. We took her out to London Airport, and I remember feeling very sad, the first of our little gang to leave home. I remember too that we went to the big restaurant at the airport, and Sarah chose the fish on the menu, but she got a bone stuck in her throat, which made me feel even more sad to see her leaving.

She took some courses in the University of Copenhagen to learn the language, which she seemed to pick up very quickly (she had always been very good at languages) and then later took classes in their architecture department, which she enjoyed a lot. The parents she was helping with their children, both worked, but did not need her on weekends, so she was able to go to stay with Ingerlise and her husband and two children. She also used to spend many weekends with Mr. and Mrs. Schelde, the parents of our friend in Newport Beach, who were very kind to her.

In the meantime we were settling back in Blackheath and Nils and Tanya were enrolled in Crown Woods comprehensive school, and Sam went to one in Blackheath village. Geoff did some teaching at the AA school, but I was busy redoing our ground floor flat, just like the old days. I changed the room in the front of the house to a new dining room, and redecorated everywhere. Life back in London was really hard after all the conveniences of our life in the States, parking was impossible, and my Volkswagen Camper was too high to fit into a number of car parks, especially Sainsbury's where I did all my food shopping. We really enjoyed seeing all our old friends in England again, and made several visits to see parents and relatives. Sarah came back for Christmas and we went up to my parent's house. After the holiday Sarah returned to Copenhagen and the January and February weather was very gloomy for us, so I found new tenants for our flat and we decided to return to Santa Barbara.

We flew back to Los Angeles, and went to stay with our friend Rita Gapp in Newport Beach. She met us at the airport. The first thing I had to do was find a new car as we had sold the Ford station wagon before we left Cima Linda. We got a local paper and started the car searching. I found a wonderful red Ford Mustang, which was old, a 1965, and it was the car I wanted to buy in Albuquerque when we first came in 1967 but with all six of us it was too small. I saw them around, it was a convertible, and in California you can have the top open, most of the time.

We returned to Santa Barbara with no house to move into, so we stayed for a short time on the beach at the Miramar Hotel, while we searched for rentals. We found a house on Roble Lane, on the Riviera, and were able to sign a lease for one-year. It was a good house to return to, it was large enough for us as Sarah was not with us. It had a big deck overlooking the whole City and ocean beyond, so at night it was quite dramatic, and I loved the views, very exciting all the time.

February 1974, we settled back to our friends and schools for the children. Sarah came over from Denmark to visit us in the summer of 1974 and she had decided she would like to return to London. I went over to Spencer House in the summer to fix up the top floor flat for Sarah to return to and live in with a group of students.

We had had another Sarah, the daughter of Lois and Peter Day living in that flat and she had found other students to share with her. I wrote to her several months earlier to say that I would need the flat to be vacant when their schools finished for the summer. Unfortunately when I got back I found we had 'squatters', the laws made it almost impossible to get non-paying tenants (squatters) to leave. One of the boys in the flat had met two Scottish lads who had come to London for a big soccer game and had nowhere to stay so they had told them they had room in their flat. There were two very large spaces, like small rooms in the angle of the roof, off the living room and they had moved in there and got a mattress on the floor. One of the front rooms was padlocked, and the boy, who had been there, had gone on vacation to Greece and left all his belongings locked in that room, which was the one I needed to fix up for Sarah.

I got my old builder Len Earl around to change the locks to that flat and the two boys in the storage space, left straight away. I still had the problem of the boy who had gone to Greece and wondered when he was likely to return. I got Len to take the padlock off the door as I needed to start work on all the rooms.

That flat had always been rather cold, because it was the top fourth floor and got all the north winds from across London. I decided to get some double-glazing for the Windows and to insulate the ceiling and walls with sheets of insulation foam. I had picked up our Volkswagen camper from my parents so I was able to collect materials and order double-glazing and pick it up in a DIY (Do It Yourself) store in Bromley. I got big rolls of foam, which I glued on to the plaster on the ceilings and outside walls.

I moved a bed for myself into the big living room as that was in the best condition. One night while I was sleeping, I had a tremendous shock! I was woken up by a huge crash—the old original hair plaster ceiling had fallen from the laths, it must have been hundreds of years old and was very heavy. It hit a lamp on my bedside table, which exploded the bulb, and the weight of all the plaster pinning me down made it difficult for me to get out of bed!!

Another night I was woken again by loud banging on the door to the flat, and it was the boy returning from Greece. I went down and called through the door to him that all his belongings were out on the landing, and he should take them away. I was lucky that he didn't return with the police because at that time you could not evict squatters this way.

Peter and Alison Smithson, good friends of ours, had bought a country house to fix up for the family to use for holidays. They drove down from London to find their house occupied by squatters. Peter decided to evict them legally, which meant hiring an Attorney and taking them to court. In the meantime the squatters stayed in their house. It took him about six months and quite a lot of money to get possession of his own house. The 'squatters rights' were the most ridiculous law, I cannot believe anyone in their right mind would allow somebody who broke into your house to remain there. I always worked on the premise that if they wanted to sue me for throwing them out, I would by then be back in America and none of them had the money to go to court against me, anyway.

It was a fun Project to be fixing up and furnishing the top floor flat. It was the most exciting of our flats because it had wonderful views right across the whole of London with the view of Saint Paul's Cathedral and Westminster standing out of the whole panorama.

I went out to the Habitat store in Bromley and found some very good plates, bowls and cups etc and a set of cutlery and pots and pans. I bought towels for Sarah and sheets, and I guess I must have bought her a bed. Carpets, for the floors, and a few nice pieces of antique furniture. I was very pleased with the way it all turned out.

Although I was very tired at the end of each day it was fun to go out to meet old friends in the evening for dinner. Tom and Pam Margerison (Tom was from our University days, and the friend who had shared my flat in Chester Square, all in my first book) invited me over one evening. They lived in Dulwich, I had to go through Lewisham and round the traffic island in Catford where my town hall had been planned, and I swung around the one-way street, and was amazed to see my building was suddenly there, it had been built by them!! Unfortunately they had made one very sad change to my design, the ground floor windows, which had been floor to ceiling glass, with sheer curtains to let in the light to the conference rooms, had been changed to a solid wall up to about two feet from the ceiling, and then little high windows above that, it had a typical council look! None of my friends had ever written to tell me it was being built, so it was a tremendous shock to see it!! I think I drove round the island several times, I couldn't believe my eyes.

On my last evening before returning to California, my old boyfriend from University days, and good friend David Allford asked me to go with him to a very special dinner in a restaurant in Hampstead, where each course was to be prepared by a different, famous chef. By that stage I was so tired from all my work, and when I was tired I lost my appetite. I felt very bad to only peck at each new course. The chefs were all carrying their very elaborate dishes round the restaurant for us to see, before they served it, and there were so many courses. I think a very simple meal I could have managed better. David was telling everyone afterwards 'I never took out such a dud bird!'

I was really pleased to get back home to Santa Barbara as that had been an exhausting trip and the slow pace of a smaller town really suited me better.

We knew that by February 1975 we would need another house as the old people who owned the Roble Lane House wanted to retire to Santa Barbara. I started in good time to search to find a house that we could purchase, as continually renting did not really suit me. I found an old house downtown that I realized could be fixed up easily for us. It was on a corner lot, a strange house as the French door entrance was from Olive St directly into the living room, but it had another French door entrance on the side, on Figueroa, that went into the dining room, so one of the first things I did was put a fence round the front garden. We stopped using the entrance into the living room, and built a good deck in front of the French doors, so it was a very private place to sit out.

The paint on the exterior of the house was very poor so I decided to re—paint it myself. I did work on the garden too, and we built a lovely deck off the back bedroom into the back garden, this was from Tanya's room. I changed the bathroom to make it more modern. It was quite a comfortable house with hard wood floors and I was lucky that we were very near the Senior high school so Tanya and Nils could walk into classes. I had to drive Sammy, as he was in Cleveland school.

It was then at that stage on his first day in school he met one of his very best friends, an English boy whose mother was Welsh and whose father was a black photographer in New York. Jason and Sam became the best of friends. They really got into surfing, so I would drive them to the beaches with the good waves for small guys. Recently Sammy at 40, was able to contact Jason again, after losing touch for years, and they all went to Mexico on a surfing trip together, and stayed in a very good house that Sammy had designed. He had studied Architecture at Sci Arch in Los Angeles. It is an excellent school, the nearest thing we have found in the US to the school where Geoff used to teach in London, the Architecture Association.

I began to think how lovely it would be to have a house up in the hills above Santa Barbara, to have more open space and to be in a quieter area. I started slowly looking around for some nice district, and one day a real estate person took me to see a house on Coyote road, in Montecito. Friends told me they would never buy next to the rather infamous neighboring house, an old adobe I was very intrigued to see the adobe for myself, so I wandered down the drive and was delighted to see how much character the adobe had. It had one long wing, which was entered up some wooden steps and then a low wing, all built in adobe bricks, around a center court. That lower wing had a very nice family in, and the father was there as I walked down the drive. He showed me around a little, it was rather a ruin. He said they had been trying to sell it for a long time. I took Geoff up to see the house (once again it was 'over my dead body' which, if you remember, was the same when I bought Spencer House) A good friend Gary Peters came up with us, he was a real estate agent. The owners did not want to use any real estate people, so we took Gary along as just our friend, to help us negotiate a deal. The house was in need of a tremendous amount of work. Here is a photo after we had rebuilt it.

As well as the main house there was a small separate cottage and a guesthouse. On the back porch open to the skies, with no walls, they had a shower. The first thing we needed to do was to make ourselves a bathroom inside and get all the rooms cleaned enough to move into. We sold our house downtown for twice the amount we had paid for it, which was surprising as I had spent very little to make it charming, I guess the work I had done really paid off.

We were terribly lucky, one Saturday I noticed in the paper that somebody was advertising 'building materials', we knew we would need a lot of materials. It was the old Dabney family estate, on Ontare road. There was a little old guy, I guess he was the caretaker of the large estate which had not been occupied by the owners the Dabney family, since the 1920s. The main house was like the movie of Miss Havisham's house in 'Great Expectations', it had huge vast rooms and every room was hanging in giant cobwebs and quite eerie to see. He explained the whole house was to be demolished for a new housing development, and any of the materials we would like, we should give him some prices of what we would pay for them.

The living room of the house had the most beautiful French doors with fanlights over, all the way down one side of the room, so we said we would certainly like those, they were from Portugal and had the slightly wrinkly old glass and amazing brass locks and door hardware that could be polished back to life. The same room had a massive carved stone fireplace, which he said was imported from Portugal as well, so we added that to our list. The house that we were buying had very poor windows everywhere, but it was such a strong old character, so we decided anything we did to it should tie into the early house, so we made an offer on many of the small windows in the main house, as well as in many of the small houses, that were all to be demolished.

We made an offer on the old roof tiles of the main house, as they had a beautiful old patina, and were really very valuable, but the people rebuilding the Presidio, a landmark downtown outbid us on those. In the garden we found a fountain that we got, plus a lot of beautiful old paving bricks.

Our next problem when we had our offers accepted was to decide how to get all the materials out, before the demolition people started on their main work on the various Dabney properties. I know it must have been a vacation time because Nils and his friend Brad Sellentin were able to work on it for us. Nils took a chain saw and knocked a hole through the wall around the beautiful French doors, and just sawed them loose. He was even able to get out the threshold piece of wood complete, so the whole thing was ready to put straight into another new wall.

Getting the fireplace out was our most difficult job as the stone pieces were so large and heavy and could not be lifted. I got a local Danish builder, Bud Bredall, to bring a hoist and tackle and they were able to throw a chain over some of the beams, and lift off the large stones, piece by piece. It was a beautiful cut stone fireplace, also originally from Portugal.

Once we could move in, we were able to start on the most important projects. We got a comical English plumber to install a shower, as we urgently needed a quick bathroom. The main wing of the adobe had an open porch along in front of all the small rooms, which were to be the children's bedrooms. Each of their rooms had a small wood-burning stove, as there was no heat, so we left those for a while. The large room at the end of the galleria had to become the living room plus our bedroom.

It seems we have been doing projects on the house ever since! Geoffrey did all the drawings for a new big living room, over the low single storey adobe on the lower level. We got a structural engineer Frank Hodosy, to design our supports for the new big room, we had to cut through the adobe walls below, and insert new concrete columns into the ground, up to the level of the new 2nd floor. Frank then designed a flexible connection from the top of the columns on the new 2nd floor, they are multiple two by sixes nailed together and surrounded by plywood, nailed every three inches. I was able to find some massive beams down in Ventura, nearby, they had supported a bridge and now span the new living room, from the columns on either side of the room. Again Frank the engineer, gave that joint a flexible connection, huge bolts were slotted in holes through the beam. They are held by ears, on the top of the column. It has been through a few earthquakes, so I think he had some good ideas. Frank designed a slab support to go in over the bathroom downstairs, and that was the base for the very hefty fireplace.

We were lucky, we were able to get Bud Bredall and his team in to build the room for us, we had all the materials from the Ontare, Dabney house, even the boards of the ceiling they were twelve inch wide old boards. We used some of the adobe bricks we had taken out of the kitchen walls to make new windows there, and we surrounded our chimneystack with those, and two of the windows have a low adobe wall below them, with the same adobe bricks. The plan was to tie the new living room visually into the old parts of the house, by using old materials. I found a floor from an old gymnasium in Santa Maria that was bird's eye maple, so I bought all of that and had it delivered, but we didn't have anyone to install it.

Sarah decided she would like to come over from London for her 21st Birthday party, November 24th 1976, so we decided that I should get going laying the floor myself. It was all tongue and groove boards, about 2 ins. wide, so was very slow going. Some of the boards were not exactly straight, so I cut a small piece from one board, with a good groove in it so I could slide it along, and really whack at them without damaging their tongues to get them to be a very snug fit. I remember Tanya and Sam helping out too. Nils was away with Brad I think on one of their travels.

The rooms below the new living room, we changed into two large rooms with one bathroom. This was where Sarah stayed when she came out to her party in November. We invited many of her friends from San Louis Obispo and many of our new friends in Santa Barbara. It was a wonderful room to have a big party in, the dimensions of the room are forty-six feet overall length, by twenty-five feet, and the open ceiling has a height of seventeen feet to the ridge. Perhaps it was a love of our huge living room in Spencer House that made us want a big space, and of course California is an easier climate for heating big rooms.

In the summer of 1976, Nils was planning a surfing trip with his friend Joel down to Mexico. We had some English teenager friends visiting us in the early summer, and while they were here they had bought a rather nice VW camper van, they stayed with us for a while and after they left I found the pink slip (ownership papers) for the van in our upper car park. Their plan was to drive across America and then return to England from Washington DC. They telephoned me from the Midwest to tell me how their trip was going, and I was able to tell them I had found their pink slip for their Volkswagen. They said they didn't need it and to throw it away, but I knew they could not sell the van without it, so I hung onto it.

The next thing we heard from them they were in Washington near the airport trying to sell their Volkswagen camper, so they were phoning to see if I still had their pink slip, and I said yes I did, and the car salesman spoke to me to ask if I would send it to him after they left. I remember it was a Saturday afternoon and Nils was out on top of the roof, nailing boards on our new Living Room roof, when they phoned and I called to him 'I'm sure the car dealer would be offering them a very small amount of money as they had no pink slip'. Because Nils and Joel were going to be leaving for their surfing trip to Mexico, the camper would be the ideal car. I telephoned back to the car dealer and asked if the English teenagers were still there, they were, so I asked them how much he was offering them for their car and it was a very low price, so we arranged to get Nils and Joel over to Washington straight away to pick up the car from them, they were leaving back to England the next morning.

Nils telephoned Joel and told him the news and asked him if he could come to Washington that afternoon and help drive the car back to California. Joel's parents were out, but he said he would leave them a note and it would be fine! I drove them down to Los Angeles airport. Their flight had to change in Chicago, and they must have both been dozing, because Nils said when they were circling over Chicago, he woke up and couldn't think where they were, or what they were doing!

They first drove to Virginia to our friends Ken and Jean White, as the camper had not been serviced in ages, so they got the work done while they stayed there. They then drove straight across the states with no stops; I think it took them two and a half days—one slept while the other drove!

Nils had several scary adventures around this time. He set off with Joel for their surfing trip to Mexico in their new VW camper. I asked him to periodically phone us, so we knew where they were. After they had been gone for four or five days, about the time they would be down as far as La Paz, where they planned to take the ferry over to the main land, there was news that a huge hurricane had hit La Paz, killing over three hundred. I kept hoping we would receive a call from them, with news, but there was no power for any broadcasts, and no telephone contacts to any phones there. I finally found a ham radio operator in La Paz, who told me how devastating it was, so I asked him if he saw any boys from the US, with a VW camper, to let me know. Still, I had no word. Then I found the Governor of California was at the airport in LA on his way to La Paz, so I was able to phone him and ask him if he could locate them among the visitors to the town and let me know on his return. More waiting for several days, so I decided the best thing was to throw myself into a project, and started work on the lower floor here, as Sarah was coming out for her 21st Birthday in November and I wanted to have the bedroom redone for her—I also wanted to keep occupied, so I had something to think about. A lot of our friends kept phoning to see if we had heard from them. On the Sunday afternoon, I finally got a call from Nils, they just arrived on mainland Mexico!

Nils was telling me how amazing it all was, just after they arrived in the town, the hurricane hit, and it washed out many of the houses in the town. Nils and Joel drove to an inland beach, and faced the front of the camper to the wind. One of them tried to step out, but the sand was blowing so hard it almost cut their skin.

After the storm had abated, they drove over to the point the ferries leave from. But were told there were no ferries. There was a crowd of people waiting to leave, who were asking Nils for water and food, so Nils and Joel returned to the beach to wait in safety. The next day they went again to check the ferries, but still nothing sailing, but a bigger crowd than ever were there and they were out of fuel. I think the next day as they drove up, there was a ferry just leaving but it was packed with people. The shipping company said they were putting on another ferry, so Nils and Joel were able to escape on the next one.

When they returned to Santa Barbara we were surprised to see the front of the VW was sandblasted, and each of the wheels had lost the paint on the side facing the wind!

FIRE IN 1977!

One day in late June 1977, we were having an amazingly fierce Santa Ana wind. It was late afternoon and I was working out in the garden trying to tie up my tomato plants, before they all blew down, Geoffrey was in the kitchen chopping potatoes for chips. Nils had gone up north surfing with his friend Brad, and Sam was watching TV. Sam ran out into the garden to tell me all the power had gone off, and as soon as he said it, we could smell an amazing burning smell. We ran up to the rear car park, up behind the guesthouse and there we could see a wall of fire coming directly down to us, horizontal, like a blowtorch, from the mountain area behind. We had several hoses in the garden so Sam climbed on the roof of our guesthouse and turned on a sprinkler and did the same to the new living room roof, as we did not have the finished tiles on. We had a few minutes to get things into the car.

We had a great dog at that time called Bosco so we took him with us in the car, but we had to leave our ducks, and also a bunch of kittens and their mother who was Sam's. I had a drawer full of photographs of the children when they were small so I grabbed that, and Geoff said he had grabbed our toothbrushes! (which we discovered later, turned out to be my make-up bag, the last thing I needed) Geoff, Sam and I got out of there quick. Nils had left his new camper van in our driveway, as he had gone up north in Brad's car, but there was nothing I could do as I was the only driver that was here, we had to leave the V.W. to face the fire.

We first went north up Coyote Road to Mountain Drive and from there we could look down on the fire as it roared down our canyon. The wind was so strong and the flames were being driven horizontal to the ground, so you could see it was impossible for firemen to get in front of it to try to stop it. A large borate bomber made several drops of fire retardant down our canyon, before it was too dark to fly so low, but already the fire was too wild. We drove back down the main Coyote road, to our side road, and I thought I could move Nils' camper, but our little road was already engulfed in flames, it was not possible to return.

Our friend Gary Peters was living on the Mesa, in a house that looked over Santa Barbara into our direction so we decided to go there and see where the fire would go. He sent out for a takeout dinner and after we had eaten some, we went over to a good vantage point, and someone there had a walky-talky and they were talking to a fireman on our little road. We heard that all the houses at 740 (our number) had gone. The fire was still roaring down to town, at the bottom of Sycamore Canyon it turned along Alameda Padre Serra, destroying many houses there, then the wind changed slightly and the fire started back up north, up Las Alturas and went up to the top. It was incredible to see, the gale from the mountains was still really wild, eucalyptus trees with all their oil were exploding in flames, and gas tanks were exploding too and four hundred houses were lost.

Our good friend, Hattie, was living in her Hope Ranch house and as she had room for us to sleep, we went there. Nils had left his small VW outside Brad's house and they had gone in Brad's car, so I left a note on Nils' to tell him we had heard all the houses were gone, and not to risk going in to try to save anything.

When we got to Hattie's I was not able to sleep, as we had just heard we had lost everything, I was busy making plans for what we should do the next day. I had my Visa card and decided we should go and buy some clothes, and buy airline tickets for a vacation with my parents in England, away from any possibility of fires! Geoffrey in his old unconcerned way was asleep immediately he put his head on the pillow. I went out about 2:30am, back downtown, to see if Nils' car was still there, and it was, with my note still on it. I thought that they must have gone straight from the surfing trip up to our house, as they could hear on their car radio apparently, exactly where the fire had started, at the top of Coyote.

I had told Nils earlier in the evening of the plan Sam and I had, to go downtown to a film, and of course Geoff would have been in the house on his own, and as he can't drive, he would have been trapped, so Nils thought it was essential to get back in. They had had to approach on foot along Mountain Drive, as Sycamore Canyon was all burning and closed. They reached a police roadblock, but watched some people being allowed through, as they said they had animals to rescue, so Nils and Brad went up and told them they had to save our animals.

About 4:30 am I was finally asleep, and Hattie came in to wake us, and to tell us that Nils was on the phone and he and Brad were at the house which they had managed to save!! Our drive up there was like the worst war scenes you had ever dreamed of, isolated chimneys were all that remained of all the houses. Every plant and tree was black, and burned, grey smoking ash was everywhere. It was amazing to drive up our little road and see the remains of every house except one, our beautiful house was still there!! The bedroom end of the main house had had the roof and windows burned, and also the creek end of the new Living room was damaged. Every tree was gone except for the big redwood. (It later dawned on us why the fireman had thought we had lost all the buildings, we had had the '740' number at the end of our driveway, in front of our neighbors house, and he had lost 3 houses, everything)

I had just brought a gas mains line up our little road, to get rid of the ugly gas storage tank we had had at first, and the pipes to the house, were plastic and were still uncovered in their trench, in the ground, so the fire had ignited those and they had acted like a blow—torch on to our bedroom wall of the house, which was an adobe wall. Luckily when Nils got in he knew where the gas meter was, and was able to turn off the gas.

A lot of windows were broken, and the smoke and ash was everywhere. We had to stay in the house as the police warned us there would probably be looters in the area. Our crazy little guest house, which is all wood and partly a wood shingle roof was still all there although a huge pine tree, which had overhung the roof, had gone, and burned the pine needles on the roof. One of the firemen said to Nils, we must be a very religious family!

Nils' 2 Vespa machines were trickles of melted metal, and his VW camper had its rear lights melted, as they had been facing the fire. Nils and Brad had put our very large new oriental rug from the living room, into their car, along with our new TV—they were all ready to make a dash.

I was so pleased and grateful to Nils and Brad who were able to come in and save the house. The new master bedroom eaves had been on fire when they arrived, and there was no water to put it out, but they convinced a four wheel drive fire truck with a spray cannon to push up the road and get into the center drive to spray it's water load. Luckily I had just had a large load of mushroom compost delivered in the driveway, which was very wet, so Brad passed bucketful's of that to Nils on the roof, Nils smashed the old roof tiles to put the compost on the boards. Luckily Nils had been VERY inventive as always, to save the house.

For a while we had no services at the house, no water, electricity, telephone or gas, and it was very hard to get in and out, as the National Guard had been called in to stop people who were not residents from entering the area. A few of our friends brought us some dinners, I remember when Hattie came with food, she said straight away that she thought it was the greatest thing to happen to us, she said we could never have cleared the whole area of the brush, which is so flammable, and so prolific, and certainly the whole area was then barren, and so I was later able to take the opportunity to plant a completely new landscape on our property, and also on the bank on the other side of the creek. There was nothing to hold the bank from sliding, during the rain season.

As we had no telephone, I never thought that people in Europe would have heard much about our disaster. When I was downtown one day I decided to phone Mummy and Daddy, and tell them we had had a fire. When I got thru to them they were so relieved to hear my voice, as they had seen the whole fire on television, and had tried to phone us many times, but the stupid operator had told them there was nobody left in this area, that it had all gone!

Sarah and Tanya were both in Europe at the time, Tanya was staying with Dieter and Odile Ackernecht, our old friends from Cal Poly, and Sarah had gone over from London to Copenhagen to visit Mrs Schelde. I thought straight away that they also must be very worried about us, so I phoned Mrs Schelde, and she said 'Do you know what time it is here? It was my only chance to phone as I seldom went out, as it was so hard to get back in, I think it was probably about 4am.in the night in Denmark!! Tanya I couldn't phone as I didn't know where she was, but she had been to a party and someone there had told her that we had had such a huge fire.

Nils and his friend Brad did a navigation course, in Santa Barbara. They went off to crew with Skip Cole in his boat. He wanted to go down the coast of Mexico, but once they got to the Mexican areas there were heavy weather conditions, with no lights on land and Nils could already see that the depth finder was not accurate and not working well enough. They told Skip it was not safe to sail there, that they should return to Santa Barbara.

The next adventure for him was in 1977, he and Brad decided to go down to New Zealand. They stopped in Hawaii, and stayed with Joel who was living there, and surfing. Their next stop was Pago Pago in Samoa.

In the harbour there was a huge schooner being rebuilt, in the middle of the bay, so they found a small boat to row out to it, and found two men from the east coast who had sailed down to Tahiti in their own boat, and seen this beautiful old Brigantine schooner, Varua, in the harbour, looking very sad and neglected. They found the owner who had sailed it from his shipyard on the east coast, round the Cape. He had married a Tahitian girl and settled there. His boat had not been sailed for about ten years, but the two Americans negotiated a lease with him, and patched the hull and sailed it up to Pago Pago. They were trying to repair it themselves, but Nils could see they needed someone more knowledgeable to do all the final work. One of them was a medical doctor and the other was a wealthy east coast businessman.

They were pleased to get the offer. Nils and Brad found a place to live in Pago Pago, with the village Bakers. Nils said every time they went there they were all eating. No wonder the Samoans, are such big people!

The Varua was stripped down to the iron frame and had been reclad with new timber. The masts had to be re set and all the rigging installed and there was quite a lot of metal work to replace, the brass bar that was the one for the sails to traverse from one side to the other. Nils and Brad had great photos of all the projects they worked on. Nils, with swimming trunks on, and a huge apron to protect him from the sparks, as he did all the welding on deck.

They ordered very picturesque red sails from Hawaii. Once it was all complete for sailing, Nils and Brad sailed on Varua with one of the owners on board, and a wonderful old guy called Rupee who was a native and was also part of the crew, and they also had a cook. The other partner sailed their own boat that they had taken down there in the first place when they went to Tahiti.

Nils let me know they were setting sail back to Honolulu, and I asked him to let me know when they arrived as it looked a very long distance! He said he thought it would take about a month. He did not know at first that they would stop anywhere, but it turned out they had a week in Fanning. I imagine that would be a great break after doing the midnight shift each day, and Nils said when they went down to the cabin in the nose of the Varua it was all wet from the waves coming over the prow.

Fanning is an island in the Gilbert Islands annexed to Great Britain in 1855. Nils said they were made very welcome there, and were given one or two feasts. They were cooking sharks—and as Nils and Brad were surfing in the waters with the sharks they wondered if eating them would bring bad karma!

Rupee looks a real character, he was doing the watch before Nils and Brad, and when they were in Fanning he was showing them how to fish on the reef at night. He took a bunch of dry palm fronds and attached them round his waist up his back. He lit the ends of them and leaned over the tide pools, which attracted a lot of fish that he speared. The other thing that Nils and Brad told us about the island, there was a huge boat shipwrecked near the shore. They paddled out to it and explored it all, the engine rooms were all underwater but you could walk down a couple of cat walk levels to where the sea level was and in the eerie blue lit water see the big engines underwater. The ships log was still on board, which was odd. They brought back a really great glass porthole with a hefty brass frame.

I had worked out roughly when they would be in Honolulu, but I never heard from them, so I telephoned the harbour master and asked if he had heard anything from the Varua but he hadn't. After another ten days I phoned him again and he said the Varua had just come into the harbour and a chap with a big beard (Nils?) had gone into his office for permission to land.

They were to be in Hawaii for quite a time whilst all the internal fittings were done—refrigeration equipment etc. so Nils and Brad were planning to leave for their original destination, New Zealand. I decided to take Tanya and Sam to Honolulu to see them before they took off on another adventure. Nils booked us a place to stay in Honolulu and I rented a car so we could get around seeing the Big waves on the north shore and the other well known spots. They took us out on Varua for a wonderful sail.

It was such a perfect design of hull that it just sliced through the water leaving no wake. There were a lot of sailboats out, the strange sail design that is normal in Hawaii. Varua seemed to be the fastest boat around—with seven sails it was gorgeous!

We then flew to Kauai, the oldest of the Hawaiian Islands and I had booked us all to stay at Princeville in an apartment so I was able to cook them some good food that I knew was their favorite. Kauai was a very beautiful island, not spoiled like the main island. An old girlfriend of Brad's was working for a helicopter business and she asked if I would like to fly around Kauai, so I jumped at that. We went and hovered right up to those steep waterfalls. We went right around the island and then went down to Molokai, which is the old leper colony. There was only one poor leper still there, and he must have died since because Brad has just recently been building houses over there. He lives in Kauai, and we miss him here.

The boys flew off to Auckland for more adventures and we returned to Santa Barbara.

In January 1978, Tanya went to Boston, to help a nice family that our friend Thais Carter knew. The East coast had their worst winter weather they had had for years, all the transport was stopped and people got their skis out to get around. Tanya was amazed to have such a difficult winter, compared with the ones she was used to in California. As soon as the weather was improved, Thais took her to her country house that she had built, for a visit.

I began to make plans for our summer vacation. We had a friend who had a nice new house in Nerja, in Spain, that I was able to rent from her. Sammy and I flew to London from Los Angeles, and we went to my parents, and got out our VW camper, ready for our trip. Tanya flew from Boston to join us, and after a stay in England we booked the Hovercraft trip across to France. The VW was great for just 3 of us. Tanya's friend Chris Goena was in Paris, so we stayed there for a time in a hotel he had booked for us. Sam didn't get so many trips to Europe as the older ones, so it was good for him to start to feel at home there. We set off down the Loire valley, through all the old towns I had gone to as a student, Orleans, Blois etc. We stayed in Carcassone. It was pouring with rain, and we stayed in a camp that was under a bridge, so we didn't get soaked when we got out of the VW. The old town was really great, but we were camping in the new town, which had a real muddle of new streets. We ate most of our meals in the camper, after Carcassone we started off into Spain, and immediately the weather was great.

Sam celebrated his thirteenth birthday in Sitjes, where we had a nice hotel for a treat. We hadn't been able to buy him a card anywhere, so Tanya and I made an elaborate one on the bathroom mirror, with different shades of lipstick!! We went through Barcelona, and through the very popular coastal areas, heading down towards Nerja, which is near Malaga. One of the camps where we stopped was just near to the beach, and whilst Tanya and I cooked dinner Sam went down to the waters edge with his flashlight. After a while he came hurrying back and told us he had been flashing his light at a boat offshore that was flashing back to him. Suddenly he had seen a Spanish policeman watching him, so Sam had run back to us. We realised that there was a lot of drug smuggling on that coast, as we were not far from Morocco, so I imagine the boat was looking for their connection on land, to have their cargo collected. The following morning when we went in to pay in the office, the policeman from the night before was there, so Sam was very nervous!

Not long after that we managed to find a phone where we could phone California, they were so pleased to hear from us, as apparently a huge gasoline tanker had rolled off the road onto the campground, the one we had just stayed in, and the gasoline had blown up many of the campers. They had thought that that area would be roughly where we would be, so they were very relieved we had left there already.

We saw a lot of insane driving by some huge trucks on that trip. One had toppled off the road, way down to a field, far below the road. The drivers were very macho characters and if I passed any of them they immediately tried to catch us up and pass us. I think three blonde heads under the sunroof of our camper and a woman driver as well, seemed to annoy them!

Finally we arrived in Nerja, and found our friends house, which was very comfortable and modern. She is American, and so had got it very well furnished and well equipped. Tanya and Sam went out to wash our poor car as we had been in a lot of rain in France, and it was filthy. While they were outside a young guy came to talk to them, he was on leave from the US air force, stationed in Berlin. He was originally Cuban, and was teaching the service men judo and karate. He was very interested in Tanya, and as he was staying near to us, he came with us on all our trips.

There was a very nice beach on the coast to the East of us where we went to swim each day. We used to return into town and buy some pastries in Nerja to have with tea, on the way home. One day we arrived just when they were closing all the streets to traffic, for the evening strolling around the town. The car in front of us was the first to be stopped, but when I saw the police had the street closed we went to a side street and walked down towards the pastry shop. On our way back we found the car that had been in front of us at the roadblock, was still there.

It was a French car with one Frenchman driving. The police had explained to him that at that hour he couldn't drive through the town, but he was refusing to back up at all. There was already a big crowd gathered around, and everyone was shouting to him, but he was burying his head in a map. Finally they sent for a tow truck, which hooked up to his back end. He started his engine and when the tow truck started pulling his car back he accelerated really hard, to go forward, so the car was skidding around, left and right, burning up all the rubber from his tires. I was worried someone would get killed. After a time the tow truck gave up, the air was thick with smoke from the guy's tires. The whisper then went around the crowd that the Guardia Seville was on its way; they were apparently the top tough police of the area. We were all expecting a group of Supermen!

A small jeep type vehicle came with 4 Guardia in it. They were in rather grand uniform, but were little old guys, probably retired from Barcelona or Madrid. One of them, who seemed to be in charge got out and started rapping on the window of the drivers seat, so the Frenchman opened the door, and in Spanish the Guardia was explaining why he could not go through the town. The Guardia had his hand with a huge nobbly ring on it, on the frame of the door, and the Frenchman just yanked the door closed, trapping his finger badly, with the ring on.

By then the crowd was in a furious mood. They were rocking the car and trying to tip it over. Someone took a rock and smashed the window on the passenger side, so they could open that door. At that stage Ruben went to the driver's door, and got the poor guy to open it. The crowd was kicking the Frenchman from the passenger side, and Ruben was talking to him, I think in French. Ruben suddenly put a karate hold on the guy and yanked him out. Everyone cheered at that.

That evening Ruben and Tanya went to a dance, and Tanya said everyone was pointing and nudging someone, to show them the 'HERO' I felt quite sickened by the whole thing it was like watching a terrified animal being torn apart by people. The poor man's car was in a car wrecking yard all smashed in by the angry crowd, and he was put into jail. He told the police he was a doctor in France, and trying to go through Nerja to visit his mother who was sick. I am not sure his story was true, as he seemed a little crazy. The frenzy of a mob is certainly terrifying to see.

We drove inland one day, up to Granada, to see The Alhambra. It was a very amazing building, with beautiful Moroccan tile decorations, and wonderful gardens with water channels and pools. On the way there we had another near disaster. Our VW was very fast downhill, but slow on any climbs. I passed a small car with four guys in, on a downhill slope, but on the next climb they whizzed past us, although there were some bad corners. We came around one corner, and we saw their car had shot off the road, and was balancing on a small tree, and it was just teetering, about to drop down a steep hill.

We stopped our car at the curb, and Ruben and Sammy got out, and told the guys to open their doors on our side of the hill. Ruben and Sam clung onto the doors to steady the car, so the guys could crawl very slowly out! Ruben was certainly a good useful companion to have.

We had a very good drive through Spain and France on our return journey. We skirted Madrid, as it was such a huge city, and we took some small country roads, because the main roads were not very good, and were full of all the German and English tourists starting south for their vacations. We stopped in Pamplona, to see the famous old bullring. As there was to be a bullfight, we decided to go to see it for our first time.

It was an amazing spectacle, very colorful spectators, and very elaborately costumed matadors and picadors. The beautiful bulls when they entered were such a picture of a healthy virile beautiful animal. After that, we did not enjoy the spectacle too much. In fact Tanya and Sam being such animal lovers were very upset. To see such a powerful creature destroyed in such a short time, and dragged out of the bullring by horses, it was hard to watch.

As we drove thru the country fields of sunflowers, we had the sliding doors of the camper open, and my Spanish guitar tapes playing, and one I had bought in Paris of Edith Piaff. It was very haunting, and I loved it, but Tanya and Sam were not so keen on Piaf! We took the hovercraft back to England.

We all three returned to Santa Barbara soon after our trip to Spain. We left our VW camper back in Sheffield, with a friend of Mummy and Daddy's who was recently widowed and her garage was empty. Unfortunately, not long after we were home, she married again and moved from her house, so we could not keep our car there. Daddy managed to find a friend to drive it, and put it in a field near his house.

Unfortunately they had a terrible wet winter and the VW sank in the mud, right down to its axles. Poor daddy, these were the sort of things that worried him terribly!

Our friend Gary Peters, who was the real estate agent, who helped us to buy the adobe, managed to get a great deal from two old people for land at 999 Hot Springs road, in Montecito.

He liked the big living room we had built for ourselves at the adobe, so he asked Geoff and I to design him a new house, with the same large spaces. He and his wife Charlene had no children, so they did not plan their house for one. Not long after we started, Charlene found she was pregnant, and as we had an open space below the entrance floor level, as it was built on a slope to the Creek, we had space to add a lower floor for the new baby.

It was a very difficult site to work on, lots of big rocks all over, and we had to put in a septic system and a Leach field. I spent ages with a bulldozer guy, Sam Beresford, a real old timer, trying to find an area we could get approved for the Leach field.

The finished house was lovely and Gary and Charlene were very pleased with it. I am not sure how long they lived in it, but they negotiated with another old couple lower down on Hot Springs road and got a very good deal from them too for another lot. They sold their house at 999 for a huge profit, and it was because of that I began to think that we should find some land and build houses ourselves, without a client, as it could be very profitable.

After the successful design of 999 Hot Springs other clients contacted us. They came with all sorts of scribbles of designs they wanted, pictures from magazines and a lot of them didn't seem to have very good taste, so the idea of building our own houses was very appealing.

The first lot I found was at 227 Las Alturas, on the area called the Riviera of Santa Barbara. It had had a house on it, which was just completed before the big Sycamore canyon fire had hit in 1977. Although our house, the adobe was the first to lose a building in that fire, it had continued all the way down Sycamore Canyon, and then burnt up along Alameda Padre Serra, on the way towards the Mission. Then when the wind changed it had started back up the hill of Las Alturas and got the whole way to the top of the hill, taking out hundreds of houses including the one at No. 227.

The views from that site were spectacular, of the whole town below, down the coast and over to the Channel Islands. We had rented a house earlier on Roble Lane, which had the same views, which I loved.

Geoff and I came up with a Mediterranean concept and did all the design and drawings. I got all the permits. I found a very good old contractor to first put in the caisson foundation, as he had built them before. We were very lucky to have reduced the number we needed, as they had to go so deep. I remember two of the caissons went down about 60 feet.

Now we needed a contractor to build the house. Our oldest son Nils had worked with Bud Bredall on Gary Peters house, and also when Bud and his team had built our big living room addition at the adobe. Nils was a perfectionist on all the details. He was by this time about 23 or 24, and recently back from his two years sailing in the Pacific, on the Varua. I trusted him to be in charge of his first house for us.

I think Nils was beginning to see I needed help to keep the family going. We really had no income once we were living in Santa Barbara, and so as I slowly sold the flats in my beloved Spencer House, we were able to do some building projects for ourselves. The house on Las Alturas was the first of a series that has gone forward for many years, and been very successful in giving Nils as well as Geoffrey and me a good living.

I can't remember how long we were in the construction phase, it was a big house, three storeys on the south side, facing the ocean. As the site was so steep we went up some steps to the front door, which was the big living room level, and then down a staircase to the master bedroom. It was a lovely house, with some great features. I was able to find a gorgeous old front door, which was from Germany. It had a little glass door that opened at eye-level that had a wrought iron screen, and you could check who was at the door before opening it. I had brought a lovely series of six leaded `stained glass windows, back from one of my trips to England, and those we used on the staircase window, and all the beams and structure were in old wood, already a lovely silver grey. I must find some photos of the houses we have built here, to include in this. The dining room ceiling was wood and I painted the boards before they went up, so it was very decorative. Every room of the house had wonderful views. Here is one of my favourite photos of the living room, that's our large brass rubbing from Fellbrigg, England.

It was a difficult house to estimate the final costs, and I could suddenly see I needed more funds before the end, so I searched among the various loan offices, and got a small loan to finish it off.

The project went smoothly but when we got it finished we hit a bad real estate market. Must have been some sort of recession, but nothing was selling, although the real estate people thought the house was beautiful and they still talk to me about it. We decided we should move into it, and rent the adobe, as it is a tough old house and hard to damage, we thought. We still had Sam living at home, and as Geoff had the dining room for his office, and I had one bedroom for my office, we decided we should finish out the lowest floor, for two rooms and a bathroom.

I loved living in that house, it was great for entertaining and to work in my kitchen with those views was a real delight. One day I saw a huge Brigantine Schooner sailing into Santa Barbara, so I phoned the harbour master, to ask if it was the 'Varua' Nils' old boat from Samoa days, and sure enough it was. I phoned the captain who was the rather unpleasant guy from Nils' Pacific sailing days. Guess he had taken over and kicked out the other owner, and he was taking people on tours. I have a very sad article recently on the Varua, it is in a drydock somewhere in the northern pacific. It's for sale and needs a lot of work, again.

While we lived at the Las Alturas house we had lots of big events happened to us. First Geoff's mother came over to stay with us, with his brother Michael. Mother loved the views, as she sat out in the garden a lot, but said she did not like the lizards in the garden, "I don't like the look in their eyes!"

The next big event, Tanya had met Jim Stevenson, a veterinarian, and they got married whilst we were there. They had the wedding ceremony at a nice New England type Church on State Street, and their reception afterwards was at the polo fields. It is a lovely place for a party and we had a band and a good dance floor. Jim and Tanya had a boat in the harbour, where they both lived. We all enjoyed our trips down there as it had a good barbeque stove and we had some very good dinners with them. Amazing views of Santa Barbara as the sunsets on the ocean, and the glow lights up all the mountain ranges.

About this same time I decided we should sell off the last flat in Spencer House the one Sarah had been living in. She had met Michael Trevallion when she studied architecture for a year at the Architecture Association. I think at that time Sarah was working in Heals on Tottenham Court Road and living with him. They were married in England, then came to Santa Barbara for their honeymoon and we had a big party for them with all Sarah's old California friends, and that was another big event while we lived in the house on Las Alturas. Sarah and Mike have two daughters. Katie is now 25 and Lucy 23.

I am not sure if I have written about the flats in Spencer House being sold, one by one. One stage we had tried to sell the whole house all four flats at once, but two people in the first floor flat, refused to leave, after I had given everyone notice but these crazy pair refused, so we had to cancel that listing, which the agents Knight Frank and Rutley had produced great publicity to cover their sale by auction. I had to go over to London and I took the tenants to court, as once I was back in the house, I heard they had a dog barking, and that was against the conditions of their lease.

After all the time it took for me to get the whole house empty, we had lost the time of the Auction, so had to give the idea up. I replaced the tenants with new ones as I couldn't keep it empty. As we were still living in California, I had to keep going over every year and carry out all the maintenance, and often get the squatters out!

When the couple who had lived in the lowest floor flat (with its old wine cellar rooms) let me know that they were leaving, I went over and worked very hard again to get it all back into very good shape. As I got it finished I heard that some big houses were starting to sell 99 year leases on the different flats, and I was thoroughly tired of going over each time tenants left, and getting it back to my very high standard of finishes.

When I completed the lowest floor flat, with new covers on the furniture, everything repainted etc. the thought of tackling it all again in a few years—for the umpteenth time, I decided I must sell the lease. I telephoned the gang in Santa Barbara to tell them I intended to start selling the flats as they became empty, and they all said "please don't sell it, as we were all born there and we love it", but I said "Do you want to come back and live in it?" and they all said "no," so I went ahead and listed the 99 year lease and it soon sold.

I was very sad to gradually have to lose my great house project as I had fixed it up so perfectly and visualized in our old age we would live in our ground floor flat with the garden and my swimming pool and we would live off the rents from the other three big flats, rents are still very high in Blackheath. Now in 2011 when the whole of the world seems to have collapsed, we would have been fine with England's free health benefits and we would be back with all our remaining great friends.

What a dream I had had!

Geoffrey has not earned any money since 1972, when he was only in his forties, so we have had to use the money from my sales of flats, to bring over to do housing projects with Nils. Until two thousand and six that worked perfectly, we built some great houses between us, and when they were sold Nils and I shared the profits, which is what we have been living on. We have done a series of them now in Montecito, so I will describe those later.

I think the next flat that became vacant was the ground floor flat, Mr Sharrock and his girlfriend decided to move to the country. I returned again to England and redid that flat, which was a horrible job. They had been there for eight years at least, and were both chain smokers, so everything had a brown film over it, if you want proof of why you should never smoke, you should have tackled the clean-up I had to do. I had some very nice sheer curtains on the front of the house, and got those all down and soaked them in the bath. In a short time it looked like a bath full of strong brown tea! I had to do the same thing with all the curtains, bedding, and the upholstery, it was really depressing. I finally got that flat back to the state it was when we lived there, in fact even more beautiful.

I came back to California and not long afterwards it was sold, to a fellow who was the head of the Arts Council. We heard later that he had taken out the mezzanine we had built (in the earlier photo) in the old ballroom and installed it in the Arts Council, where he works.

The first floor flat (second floor in the United States) was sold to a Mr and Mrs Bishop, who had just returned to England having always lived abroad.

Sarah's old flat on the top floor we sold to a single woman. We had to go over to London to dispose of all the furniture we had.

Some of the things Sarah wanted to have over in their house, and the other things I advertised as a garage sale. It was very funny a lot of people came thinking they could buy a garage! They had never had garage sales, there they call them 'Car boot sales'

We finally had nowhere in London to stay, and we all came back to Santa Barbara.

We had a good offer for the Las Alturas house and sold it, we would need to find another one to buy, to live in, as we had still got tenants in the adobe,and that was working out well.

I had looked at a 50's house on East Valley Rd, several times, as it was in a good area of Montecito, but had been added too many times, so that the plan no longer worked, you had to go through a child's bedroom to get through to the Master Suite, and another large room which we later turned into a library. It had also been rented for a long time, so everything was worn out, including the garden, but it was in a good area of Montecito and priced right.

I went back there again, and realized that if we entered the house another way, through one of the children's bedrooms it could provide access to the rest of the house, we could have a nice new entrance hall, and the floor plan problem at least, was solved. We went ahead and made an offer, which was accepted.

We had been in Las Alturas for about two years, and I realized how much I had enjoyed the new house, with the most wonderful views of any place we had ever lived. As I lay on my pillow, I had views of the lights of Santa Barbara, and great views of the islands and the ocean. The big project in hand, was then to pack all our belongings into boxes, all the China, books, linens, and everybody's clothes. It was all, my job as Geoffrey very slowly packed up all the papers and books he had in his office. We had a deadline, the day that escrow closed, and that was the day we had to move into the house on East Valley Rd. So I needed to work fast.

The night before we were due to move, there was a telephone call while we were eating dinner, and whoever picked it up, said "hello Elizabeth"! It was then I realized that it must be a real crisis from England, as it was eight hours ahead of our time, so about 4:00 in morning there. When I went on to the telephone, my sister Elisabeth told me that Daddy had just died, it was October the ninth, 1984. Daddy was eighty-two years old. He had had a very bad cold, and had woken up with breathing difficulties. Mummy had gone to make him a cup of tea, which is always considered a remedy in England for most things. When she came back he had died.

I quickly phoned British Airways, to ask the times of flights to London the following day. Geoff and the children said they could manage to move all the boxes into the new house at 1705 East Valley Road. Early, the next morning I took the bus down to Los Angeles airport, and took an early flight to London. I rented a car at the airport to drive up to Norfolk, to Elizabeth's house, where Daddy and Mommy had been living. They used to divide their time between my brother David's house in Hathersage near to Sheffield, and Howard and Elisabeth's house in Norfolk.

I arrived in Reepham, Norfolk in the late afternoon, and I slept the night and the next morning when I woke up, I realised I had really wrecked up my back. I think all the packing of boxes, and lifting them into piles, had strained my muscles, and then the tension when I heard Daddy had died, followed by a long ten-hour flight to London, and then the drive up to Norfolk.

I think Daddy's funeral service and cremation were two days after I had arrived. It was very difficult for me to really believe that my long friendship with someone so vital to me was at an end. It was not for several months afterwards, that I realised how much I had depended on Daddy. I always had the feeling that I could telephone him at anytime, and from anywhere to ask for help for any of my hard decisions. I did not always follow his advice, as we were both very strong characters, and didn't agree on a lot of things. It was a feeling that he would always be there for me, if I needed him.

On my return to Santa Barbara, I went straight to our new house, which was all in a terrible muddle, with boxes half opened and things scattered all over the house. It was surprising though that they had managed as well as they had.

Geoffrey and I started straight away with the set of drawings to remodel our house. I think Nils was building a house for clients of Tommy Torres down in Malibu in the week, and returning to Santa Barbara on weekends. Sam was still in school, and I think Tanya was living with Jim on his yacht in the Harbor where she moved after her wedding.

We realized that ceilings in that style of '50s house, we found very low, there was a big living room, but with the same height of ceiling as the rest of the house. We were used to having a good height in our living rooms, after the wonderful old ballroom in Spencer House, and the living room in the adobe that we had built, and the Las Alturas house, had a very high ceiling with open beams.

As it was not possible to take that part of the roof off, we decided to lower the floor to solve the problem.

We created the new entrance hall and from there we went down to the right, two steps to the new level of the living room, and to the left of the entrance we were able to get access into a room fitted with library shelves and then beyond that into the new master suite, with new bathroom too. We still had some items left that I had shipped over from the UK, some beautiful old mahogany doors, so they went on to be the new entry into the living room. I had some beautiful plaster corbels also so we used those for the new fireplace in the kitchen.

At about that time a client called, he had an acre of land out on the eastern side of Montecito, and had just got a water meter allocation, so wanted us to design a house on it right away, so we were busy on that as well.

A little later his neighbour, a really great man Frank Bradley, who had also bought land that had just been given a water meter, contacted us, and came with his wife who was from Sweden, to see something we had designed. They were not sure at the beginning if it was to be a house for them, as they were living in Sierra Madre, in Los Angeles. We got busy on those plans too.

Frank was very honest and said he didn't have the funds to construct it, so I said if we got the land valued, he could contribute the land and we could design and build it for them at our cost. When it was complete he could purchase it from the partnership for the proportion of our costs to his. We agreed to get it valued by three real estate companies, when it was completed. If Frank decided against buying it we would have the next option, or we could put it on the market, and divide the sale price. We went to an attorney and got a very good tight contract drawn up.

Luckily Nils was free to be our contractor, and we now knew how well he built.

We really had fun building for them. A few things I phoned Frank about, we had designed French doors in the dining room, but while we were building we thought the doors would be great with fanlights (more glass) over, and we thought the room would be improved if we added a fireplace. Frank said do whatever you think will make the house better.

I still had some lovely old items from England that we decided to use. A pair of carved pine doors to enter the living room. A large, very good leaded glass half circular window, which we built into the living room wall, and a series of leaded glass windows we put together in a large panel in the master bedroom.

On several of my visits to England I had searched salvage companies in Yorkshire, Bath and London, and had been able to find many beautiful hand made items from old houses that had had to be demolished. I ended up with several shipments of very useful old decorative leaded glass windows, carved doors in very good hardwoods, and several plaster corbels and carved panels, all of which we gradually used in our various houses, and they were not items you could find in the states.

Frank and his wife Maud were so pleased with the completed house, so decided in April 1988 they would move up here from Los Angeles, and buy us out from our share. They have been very good friends to us. We visited them two summers in Melbystrand in Sweden where they have a summerhouse.

In the meantime we sold the house we had remodeled on East Valley Road to our doctor. His wife was a painter, and they asked us to design and build a separate studio for her, up in the garden. That was the next project. We were then back living in the adobe and ready to do a remodel there.

In the spring of the next year, I was about to leave to spend the summer in Europe. As I drove home to the adobe, I saw real estate signs on a parcel of land off our small road. It was a three-acre parcel, and had just been given one of the sought-after water meters. I stopped to talk to the real-estate representative to ask her for the details, and their asking price. I pointed out to her there was no access to that property from our small road, which is a private road.

I waited during the summer and on my return I found the property was still not sold, so I got the owners names from the property tax department, and telephoned them, two brothers living in Hawaii. I explained to them that they had only six months from their issue of the water permit, to turn in their building plans, or they would lose their water allocation.

I said I would be interested to purchase it, and gave them an offer of less than half the asking price. This was much more in line with current land prices in that area and they had run out of time. They said they would discuss it and get back to me. I was so pleased to hear soon afterwards that they would be happy to sell it for my offer.

As it was three acres we had the possibility to build up three separate houses, but we decided as it had such fantastic views, to build one very large elegant house, which would be a good neighbour to our adobe house. Geoffrey and I got busy designing and submitting the drawings to the County, conducting soil tests for the septic system. In the meantime while we waited for permits Nils was busy finishing the studio for our doctor's wife.

Nils got a very good team together to build the house, which turned out to be very beautiful, and for a large house on three acres, was inexpensive. We got a Real Estate company to list it, and almost immediately two men moving back from Hawaii came in one Friday and as they had all cash, wanted to close escrow the following Monday, so they could move in and have their families there for the following Thursday, Thanksgiving. I had never heard of an escrow closing so quickly, but as it was all cash, and no loan to find, the escrow company said they loved a quick escrow, as they got out all the necessary legal documents, and closed them the same day.

Nils and his friend Brad, and Sam and Kat were all living in the house, so I hunted quickly on the weekend, and found them a house to rent. I think Sam and Kat moved into our guesthouse.

David Gebhard, our good friend and a very respected architectural critic and writer, did a very complimentary article on it, which he called 'The Romance is Back'. It was in the Santa Barbara Magazine for May—June 1992.

We were very lucky to have sold so quickly as the real estate market did one of its price drops shortly after.

A real-estate friend told us there was very little land on the market, but there were two parcels on Middle Road. As we didn't know how long the recession would be, we decided to get another project to work on. It seemed a very good location, as there are several famous George Washington Smith houses there, so we bought those two lots, and decided to build one large house. Montecito has always been a very sought after area for wealthy people to live, there are some very large estates. It is a perfect place for film stars and wealthy people in Los Angeles to move to, as there are some excellent schools for children, and after the LA scene, it is an idyllic area.

We have always heard that because of the history and desirability of Montecito, and the residents from early 1840's, with their beautiful large estates, that the area was always going to bounce back, but of course there can be a long wait for that to happen, so if you can't hold the loan payments, it can be a real tough spot to be caught in.

At this stage Nils was very capable with his designs, so he decided on one or two changes to our plans and drawings for the Middle Road house. There was a very ugly power line running up Middle Road, you see a lot of them in the US, so Nils and I planned to put a large section that included our property, underground. It did not seem too expensive a project, but we had to provide underground trenching and conduit to all of the neighbor's houses as well as new electrical panels.

Our housing market was very slow to pick up, so Nils had the idea to buy a house of his own on Hot Springs Road, and whilst we waited for the market to recover, he would do a full remodel there, and live in it, in the meantime. He did a really great job and showed a very creative design sense. As it was so near the road with some traffic noise, he decided to do a water feature in front of the house. He called the home 'The Mill House' with the water source running along a high stone trough, and then spilling into a larger pool by the entry. At the spillway point is where the old mill wheel would have been mounted, turning the falling water into usable power. There was a little bridge to go over it, near the front door, and the water source continued on the back of the house. It appeared to be a natural river that had been diverted along a waterway to turn an old Mill Wheel and the remodel followed the same early time period, with a modern floor plan. Making a good falling water sound on both sides of the house. It was a very effective way to lose the traffic noise. It had lovely views from the back of the house and patio, through trees to the Montecito Country Club golf course.

The housing market was still very slow, so Geoff and I decided to move into it with a few pieces of furniture, enough for us to live with. We rented the adobe out for six months. Once we were in the Hot Springs house it sold immediately and we could not decide what to do for a place to live. I suddenly had the bright idea to have a longish stay in Europe. I telephoned the Volvo Factory in Gothenburg, and ordered a new Volvo wagon, to be picked up in Hatfield in England, on July 17th. We would use it for our whole stay in Europe. The shipping back to the states was all covered in the price. We just had to leave it back in the UK, which was fine, as our return flight was from Heathrow.

I also booked a villa for two weeks in the Chianti area in Italy, so that we would have some planned place to stay. We asked our old pals David and Beryl Allford if they would like to join us there, as they loved Italy as well.

We flew first to England, on July 1st and saw my sister Elisabeth and Mummy in Blakeney in Norfolk, and Sarah and Mike in Frome, in Somerset. As we had so long to spend in Europe, we had a car rental at first there. This gave us the impetus to visit a lot of friends in the UK. We went up to Sheffield and stayed with Geoff's brother Michael and his wife Barbara, then we went up to Kendal in the Lake District, to stay with John and Kim Satchell, our old pals from University days. They were busy with a collection of antiques. We went around the Lake District, to all the places I had enjoyed at Hunmanby Hall school, when I was evacuated to Bassenthwaite Lake, in the war. (All in my first book)

From the visit there we went down to Ludlow. A friend of ours in California had a very nice house in Ludlow, in Shropshire. I had arranged with her to rent it for a week.

My first year of Architecture studies at University, we had gone for our measuring trip to Ludlow. We had to select our late 17th century house and measure it up, so we could draw it up when we returned to University. I knew what a beautiful old town it was, with Shropshire Castle just near. There are so many wonderful unspoiled buildings there, all late 17th century, and incredibly well maintained. It was really good to see it all again.

Next stop was London, a visit to Gordon and Ursula fellow architects in Blackheath, then we drove to Benenden, with a visit to Felix and Anthea who were then living full time in their wonderful Hall House, dating from the medieval 13th century. We took the hovercraft with our new car, on August 3rd from Dover to Calais, and from there, up to Loosedrecht in Holland to stay with John and Joy Brinkworth. Lots of places round there to visit, Hilversum, Delft, Gouda, Utrecht etc. John was the friend of Geoff's from the war days, who was then a portrait painter, and had commissions from the Dutch Royal family to do their family Portraits.

We headed south from there as it was getting near the time to pick up Sam and Kat in Morcote, Lugano. I don't know how we had this energy day after day, as it is tiring to stay with so many different friends, and relatives! We stopped for two nights with Alex Charlesworth an old friend from California, who was working in Heidelburg at the time, then on to Morcote, on Lake Lugano, and Sam and Kat.

Sam was still at Sci Arch, in Los Angeles, and in fourth year you had a choice to study in one or two different countries in Europe so our period to be over there was a good time to take them with us, by car for some travels to new places.

Sam and Kat had got married in March of 1992, they had a beautiful wedding at the adobe.

Sam was a student at Southern California Institute of Architecture, in Los Angeles. They decided they would go with his school to Morcote, on the borders of Italy. The school had an overseas course in Europe for students to spend a year over there. They had a wonderful time, first in Paris, where the school did a project. Then down to Barcelona where they did another project, and then the next was in Berlin where they had bicycles and toured all around, they did one last project there. It was a very interesting experience for students from the United States to spend time living in cities in Europe. Another world from the US and California!

They then went for the rest of their stay to a rambling house the school was renting in Morcote, on Lake Lugano. What a beautiful picturesque village that is. No wonder, an architecture school from California would have chosen it for their students abroad. It had some very great architecture.

They were renting a very large tall building that housed all the students, and they had rooms for lectures and workshops. There were students from Japan who joined them, and Sam was very amused by them, he said they were bristling with cameras, and photographing everything in sight, even the food on Sam's plate, in close up!!

We were able to stay there as most students had left for their summer vacation, and they had a very good restaurant in their basement. We made tours all around, into Lugano, and saw a very good Art Exhibition there.

It was very amusing because Sam asked me whilst we were still in Santa Barbara to go out to UCSB and buy them euro rail passes, to make their criss-crossing rail trips, and send them over to them. In the United States they write the date with the month first, then the day and then the year. In Europe dates are written day of the month, then month, and last the year, so each time they used the rail pass there, the inspectors thought they were still valid, because they misread the date! Sammy always seems to get lucky on these sort of things.

We went up to the top of the mountains above Morcote, where you could look out over the Milanese plain, and see for miles.

We drove from Morcote to visit Geoff's niece, Julia with her Swiss husband, Godi. They lived in the mountainous area above Lake Geneva. I don't know if Sam had ever met this cousin before, but they made us very welcome. We went up to a mountain area, and had some very good fondue, in a bar, which Sam and Kat got treated to many times during their Swiss stay!

We headed north from there back up to Heidelburg, another wonderful architectural town, to visit Alex again, and then on up north through Germany to Lubeck, which we knew many of the famous monuments, bombed in the war, had been rebuilt. It was very impressive. Lubeck is very near to the ferry from Puttgarden across to Denmark. We drove up through Denmark and took the ferry across, the ferry that used to cross to Sweden. I think that is now replaced by a tunnel. We drove north from Malmo where the ferry delivered us, up to Melbystrand where our friends Frank and Maud from Santa Barbara, were living in their house for the summer. That was lovely to have friends there to welcome us, and it was very good to have Sam and Kat with us for this whole trip, and to have help with all the driving too! We looked around at some of the beautiful old buildings in the countryside around there. Although the Swedish modern buildings were well known in England, I don't think we were ever aware of how beautiful a lot of old country places are. We loved the way they had preserved so many of the really old places.

We had a friend in Stockholm, Gosta Edberg, an architect who had been in America and he had a small flat in the centre of the town, where we could stay. He was living in a house just to the north of the city, where we went to see him again and for some good dinners! Stockholm is a wonderful town, on the sea, and very interesting buildings. The Town Hall is very striking, and just near to it we made a tour of the Vasa. It was built in the early 1600's as the royal flagship, built to fight the Kingdom of Poland. It was a well remembered, disaster by Sweden, the fate of the Vasa.

It was a 64 gun warship, and when it was first launched in 1628, it hit a sudden squall and as she had just fired her farewell salute, all her gun ports were still open, and when she listed heavily to port, the gun ports sank below the water level, and water gushed in. It took only a few moments for her to sink. (This is very similar to what happened in 1545 to the English vessel Mary Rose.)

The Vasa is now housed in a very elegant museum, but in 1992 when we were there it was in a temporary drydock, where she was being treated with continuous sprays of polyethylene glycol to slowdown the drying process of the timbers, so they would not crack. It had been on the seabed for three hundred and sixty four years.

As we were in such a traveling mood, we decided we would sail over to Finland from there. We were warned, by people that many Swedes have an alcohol problem, and so they cannot purchase drinks in Sweden. We were never told that on Friday nights after payday, they all book these ferries as they can buy drinks. Unfortunately we had booked to sail on a Friday, so the boat was full of drunks!

When we left for Finland, it was very interesting to see all the small little islands that the boat sailed through, they were owned privately by people as a summer vacation home, and they had small sailboats anchored on their own little landings, between Stockholm and Turku in Finland. Our drive east towards Helsinki was very amazing that the small houses we passed looked so like Russia. It was particularly strong in the Cathedral Square in Helsinki. That is where they filmed 'Reds' in 1981. We knew that that part of Finland was in fact Russian at one time.

Finland has produced many world famous artists, the architect Eliel Saarinen was world famous and we did several tours of his buildings. He designed the Helsinki Railway station, which we all four went to visit. It has four very powerful statues outside, and we went into the main tearoom, and that was exactly as if we were in Russia again, a very powerful design.

We went on a tour around Eliel's very famous house, Hvittrask, 'The home as a work of art'. It was a very powerful statement of his talent, built for his own family when he was only in his late twenties, in 1900-1903. He used some brilliant crafts people to make tapestries and decorative details, lights, windows, rugs and furniture. The house was an amazing feat, set on a lake and furnished with so many pieces by such talented craftsmanship made by his friends, and his family.

In the autumn of 1922 when he had reached the age of 50 he learned he had won Second Prize in the competition for the new headquarters of the Chicago Tribune. The whole family moved to the States in 1923. Their beautiful home was left silent, but they did return every summer.

(Eliel's son Eero became an architect too, and got some very good clients in the Detroit and Chicago area. In my first book when Geoffrey was writing articles on USA architecture, he was asked to visit the new General Motors Building that Eero had just completed in Detroit. He had a very good visit to see Eero and he wrote a great article in Edilizia Moderna.)

The famous composer Jean Sibelius lived in an area near to Hvittrask, in the countryside outside near Helsinki. I really love his music, so we also went on a trip to visit his house. It was a very different scene, and had the air of sadness around the house. He must have been a very difficult person to live with, he had children, but he demanded absolute silence in the house, so he could concentrate on his composing all the time.

We booked to take the ferry over to St. Petersburg in Russia. We decided to leave my new white Volvo in a storage building, near the ferry, as we had heard that we would be likely to have parts stolen off the car in Russia. We boarded a Russian boat for the sail, it was quite a long overnight trip, but it was very entertaining. After we had had dinner in the large dining room, all the waiters, and everyone working in the kitchens put on their Russian peasant costumes, and danced many of the old Russian Country dances, and the men danced the troika as if they were the old cossaks.

On the deck at the back of the boat they had built a large wooden tank, filled with water, for a lot of passengers, who found that area was too hot, and wanted to swim whilst we were docked in St Petersburg. We returned to our boat each evening, taking a very wild taxi ride from the Port into the town each day, and a few days they had organized a tour for us, but mostly we were on our own. It was a crazy taxi ride because the streets were cobbled, and had some huge potholes, and the taxis did not want to drive slowly, I think it was a matter of pride, they wanted to prove they were all up to the American cities, so they drove fast swerving back and forth to avoid the holes!

There were some wonderful examples of their classical buildings. St Isaac's Cathedral, it is the fourth largest domed Cathedral in the world. One of the oldest and most beautiful Russian Orthodox Churches, with all the decorative little onion domes—the buildings were all very well maintained, and the gardens in front of the Hermitage Museum were immaculate. I sat on one of the garden benches there listening to a good brass band, and watching the girls pass with their children and babies, just like any Capital in the world, and the girls were wearing very elegant current city clothes. I was very impressed. We went into the Hermitage Museum briefly, but it was so vast, and the weather was so hot. It was by then September, and the countryside in that area of Russia had something like fifty fires burning, so it was very smoky.

We went down to the Neva River and took one of the evening cruises, as it was getting dark. That was delightful, on the river they were playing balalaikas on our boat, and serving very good Vodka as we sailed through the city. We returned to our ship every evening and for our return sail back to Helsinki. During the night, I got up on deck when we were on our way, as I wondered if they had taken off the strange box on the deck, to swim, but it was still there, and had some huge waves swaying up the sides as we hit some big waves on the sea.! It struck me as a very amusing effort to provide such a simple pool!

We collected our lovely new white Volvo on the docks, and transferred it to the return ferry for Stockholm. Sam and Kat needed to return from Stockholm to Morcote by train, so we took them to the station, and it was our turn to make our return trip by car, all the way south, finally down to Italy where I had rented our house in the country, near to Radda in Chianti.

We picked up our old friends David and Beryl, from London at the airport in Florence, and then headed south to find the house where we were to stay. It was beautiful, an old stone group of buildings, that had been remodeled by an Italian lady who was working in the UN in Belgium. All around us were vineyards on the slopes of the hills, and olive trees in every direction. As I had paid for the house, Dave said they would pay for all the food, and they had really gourmet tastes, so we ate at some wonderful places, and Dave always finished the meals with the grappa selection, which came around on a trolley loaded with so many different grappas, from different areas in Italy.

There were so many beautiful towns and villages around us. Our nearest place for delicious foods, was Radda. Dave went off early each morning to buy fresh bread, and lots of prosciutto—crudo, a perfect breakfast!

We were not too far from Sienna, which is a lovely architectural town, so we spent two trips there, wherever we went Dave was always buying some great delicacies.

I remember the house had no screens on the windows, which does seem crazy as we used to get scorpions in our rooms at night, and Dave and Beryl called out a couple of nights as they hid under the sheets, while I went in and killed the bugs. Screens are so easy to apply to windows, I can't think why so few places in Europe use them. We were all very cautious about scorpions.

We headed back to England, and left our Volvo there to be shipped back to us in California.

I had always sent a subscription to KCET our local PBS station, with no advertising and a good news station and programs from

England. They had been trying to contact me whilst I was away, and when I got back KCET phoned and told me the last contribution I had sent was in fact a raffle, and I had won first prize. I guessed it would be something like a new set of pans! She said it was the new SAAB Aero.

I was amazed and phoned Nils straight away to tell him. He said a lot of old people were getting these silly offers, so I doubted if it was even true.

After a short time they telephoned again and told me I had a choice of colour for the car and the seat leather, and where would I like to pick it up, so I chose Tors Saab in Lompoc nearby, and I realised it was really true!

My white Volvo arrived in early October, and the silver Saab came at the same time! I had never won anything before in my life!!

Whilst we were away Nils got back to the larger, grander house on Middle Road. The house turned out beautifully and the young lady who had bought Nils' last house on Hot Springs, fell in love with the new one, and bought it too. Her father was one of the original Pan Am Air lines owners, and he seemed very willing to help her invest in houses, and also a Store on State Street, where she sold beautiful furniture for houses. The house looks like she must have had great fun searching for special furnishings and displaying them beautifully.

We were then looking for the next project, and found a great site on Cota Lane, which is very near to the upper Village in Montecito, an area with beautiful Spanish homes from the 1920's.

Nils was just married and bought a little house on Hermosillo Drive, to start to raise his family. He was doing most of the design now, using European style buildings with authentic details designed with a California floor plan. He was able to get onto plans, drawings and permits very quickly. He designed a very interesting house, and proceeded to build it very quickly. He bought the land, designed, built and then sold the house, within a year and we had a big Birthday Party for me there, June 10th. Good healthy economy in those days, unlike today, 2011.

Next, he found a great hill top property on Hot Springs Road, in Montecito, for our next project together, which sold quickly.

He then found a good site on East Valley Road, which is nearer to the centre of the Montecito Village, and right in the heart of the Old Spanish buildings. It had an old tumbledown house on it, so Nils first cleared the site, and designed a beautiful house.

The plan of that one was perfect, you entered large gates, under an entrance arch, into a good sized patio, on the left were the garages, and on the right side of the court was the main entrance, and on the far side of the house was a very private courtyard garden, with terraces opening onto the court. The style of his houses was a Mediterranean Spanish or Italian design, which in our climate is very appropriate.

Nils arranged a big party for the opening, he had a Spanish guitarist playing in the inner courtyard, and food catered by Pane Vino. It was a perfect warm evening and the house looked at its best. One of Nils' friends was also a real estate man, and he knew the ideal couple in San Francisco who were wanting to move into a classic house and he got them to come down immediately, and they bought it. It never really went on the market, and a number of real estate agents complained to me, they never got in to see it!

Nils then moved up to a much larger site on Buena Vista Avenue, in Montecito. This is a very good address, quiet and wonderful mountain views. It was the grandest house that he had designed and built, he puts so many hours of additional work into all his projects, and it always makes for a remarkable home for someone. Perfect details and craftsmanship, I am very proud of his work.

I've always enjoyed watching the projects progress. It gives me the feeling of really achieving something, then producing a great end product.

Two disasters combine in 2007.

The USA has suffered a huge loss in house prices and economies around the world have been affected due to the American Banks. They gave larger and larger mortgages to people who did not qualify for such big loans. In 2006 we were told by some good economists that we were in for a BIG CRASH.

When this happened we were just finishing our biggest and most expensive house on Buena Vista. I heard the economist, Nouriel Roubini talking to Charlie Rose in 2006, warning of the crash, so I told Sam and Nils we should get our current houses on the market quickly as the prices were still very high in Montecito. Sam sold the house he had built for himself, for a good price, and decided they would start renting instead. Nils wanted to put the finishing touches to the Buena Vista house. When we did put it on the market, house prices were dropping rapidly. Nils held the house for a year, which was very expensive. Finally in 2007 it sold, for much less. Ever since that time many houses have gone into foreclosure, as the value of houses has dropped below the cost of the mortgages.

The other disaster, locally in Santa Barbara, we have had a Huge Brush Fire.

On November 13th 2007, our daughter Sarah and Greg who now live in Cornwall, England, flew over to visit us in Santa Barbara. The day they arrived we sat in the garden having tea together when suddenly a very powerful Santa Ana wind sprang up; it was almost blowing the china plates off the table, so we had to rush our tea inside the house.

A little later I was starting to prepare dinner and Geoffrey was looking out of the glass kitchen doors that look to the north of the house, up to the mountains and said there is a wonderful red sunset over there. I knew it could not possibly be a sunset in the north so I went out and saw flames coming high behind the top Guesthouse. Those Santa Ana winds are so strong so they push fires at a very fast speed. We grabbed our pills and left! Sarah and Greg followed us in their rented car, down to Sam and Kat's.

Sam and Kat luckily were renting a house in lower Montecito, well away from the fires, so we all went there. Sarah and Greg were in a motel downtown. Nils had room in his house so Geoff and I decided to sleep there.

Meanwhile the Santa Ana still roared, so we knew we were going to be out of our house for a long time, but we didn't realize quite how bad the fire was going to be and how it was going to affect us.

After dinner at Sam's we drove up to a hill where you can overlook our road, which we could see was all a blaze. We were not allowed to get too near by the police cordons, and we could see it was already burning in the west areas towards Goleta.

I returned to Sam's house feeling very exhausted by the whole thing. I think I realized, the fire combined with the economic downturn was going to be very tough going at 85. I had also counted on the value of our Coyote property, with all the improvements we had made over the years. After the housing crash the value was reduced to 50% and then the tremendous impact to our neighborhood from the fire damage, we were now down to one third of the value of just a year ago.

The next day the police let us through their cordon, as we were desperate to see what was left. Everything in our little road was completely gone. One house that Sam and Kat had recently built very well, Kat had done a great garden on the banks of the creek and they had no brush around, that was all still there, and probably the reason that house was fine. Higher up the road we circled down our drive, most of that planting was gone, but miraculously the main house and the studio stood there proud!

All together the fire that had swept along the mountains behind us to the west, took out two hundred and forty houses in one night. They are really terrifying, as they go so fast driven by the wind, and the firemen can't seem to get in front of them to hose the structures.

The police were able somehow to find the ten college students who had started the fire. They had climbed over high fences posted with 'No Trespassing' and 'High Fire Area' signs and gone up to the old Tea House and partied and built a campfire. Unluckily one night later the Santa Ana winds blew and took the hot ashes to the dry brush all around.

We were the only house around, surviving in our part of the road and there was no power anywhere, but Sam and Nils had generators so we were able to run a few lights in the house, and one car was left parked outside the garage. The police always go round and warn people there are prowlers around after a fire coming in to steal things, if nobody is there.

We stayed at Nils' house for several nights, but we all went up in the daytime and took new hoses to water the smoldering ashes that were everywhere. We couldn't believe our luck the fire had climbed up a Bignonia Cherere plant I had had climbing up to the balcony outside the living room and that had swept a fire up to the end French doors and burned the window screen. I have a feeling one of the firemen I know had gone in and hosed that down, and he had left a hose running on the back of our huge redwood tree, as the outer bark had caught fire near the ground. I know our two boys had gone in during the night. Nils has a big truck and he has a flashing red light he can put on top of the cab, and so looked like an official.

My good friend in the Fire Department knew how valuable our house was to us, and how hard I had worked to get it so perfect, so he suggested to me in the Spring of 2007 that our creek was really dense with brush, so it may be best to get it cleared. I got a team of guys with chain saws to cut everything and to cart it all away. Something had saved us once again! But unfortunately it hadn't worked for the guesthouse. It was a very charming two bedroom little house, and north of our main house. I had taken the wood shingles off the roof, and put a metal roof on, which was lying on the ashes, but the fire had got straight into the walls. That was a waste of money for what was supposed to be a solution!

We gradually got the gas lines repaired and got the electric company to replace the power pole, and run new wires down to the house and then we could move back in.

Lots of clearing of burnt dead trees and plants which is always very expensive, and in the meantime when two hundred and forty plus houses are struggling with our same problems or worse- the District Attorney handling the arsonists decided they couldn't be sure if their fire or someone else's had started the blaze, and let them off!! We, and our neighbors, really felt betrayed by this outcome!

All of this and the disappointing sale of Buena Vista had brought us to 2008, but it is now 2011 as I near the end of this book. I still can hardly believe my fears in 2006, for America's future, are actually happening. I know Nils is really struggling to bring new development costs under control his recent project just sold and gives some hope for the future.

The poorly regulated global financial system - much of it in the USA - brought the whole world economy crashing down. First it was the banks in Iceland who had been investing in our banks. Now the only European countries that are still stable are at the top-Norway. They found oil in the North Sea, which the UK was partners with them in bringing up that oil. Denmark is the next stable economy and then Finland, Australia and New Zealand, and Sweden is the sixth.

They have sound currencies because the banks did not tempt unqualified buyers with loans at very low rates, which tempted all the speculation, and brought about the total US collapse. Mortgage Companies here went Bankrupt, with their debts bought by several US banks.

The bankers have created world wide chaos, and when they were called in to answer in Congress about their practices, the CEO's said they knew they had a lot of troubled loans on their books so they packaged them and sold them to their clients, and then proceeded to bet against them!

This would seem to me to be a criminal way to conduct business, but I was told that there is no law against it, and so none of the bankers have gone to jail- they have been allowed to get away with terrible behavior, and the Government has bailed them out with our taxpayer's money! The banks then proceeded to give bonuses to their own top executives!!

Montecito had come to the forefront in being one of the most desired areas of the country, partly because of the warm climate year round, and the fact that we still have wonderful old houses from a very affluent past. We have many billionaires living in Montecito, and the land prices had sky rocketed.

The past twenty years our development business was doing well, but the economic down turn hit Montecito with a 50% fall in property values. The impact on our business and real estate holdings is severe.

In 2007 the US Banks greed and dishonesty caught up with them. This destroyed the US economy and sent real estate values tumbling across the Country.

President Reagan was responsible for removing the checks and balances on US Banks and US financial institutions. It took less than thirty years for US Banks to self-destruct without the necessary Government controls.

On top of this financial problem, the US has the influence of special interest groups always getting in the way. This creates an inability to do the right thing. This is not a Democracy. The US political system unfortunately seems to be too driven by money and greed.

I Wrote my cousin in New Zealand recently to see if things were more hopeful there, and also if he had any suggestions for the end of this book. I had heard their economy was doing surprisingly well. Nils had been down there on a surfing trip, and then Sam and I had also toured both Islands and had liked it. I asked Geoff, what about New Zealand at eighty-five? He had the same response to when I showed him Spencer House "Over my dead body!" so it seems hopeful!

My dear June,

Ever since your last email a couple of weeks ago I have been wondering what to say in reply. You certainly brought us up to date with your situation, and it's a gloomy picture. The obvious thing is to write in a platitudinous way, equivalent to patting your back and saying, "There, there." But that won't do.

We have to face it, we somewhat more mature people, that the world has gone backwards since we were young. We're in good company: People have been saying it for thousands of years. Admittedly, I think the USA is in for a difficult ride this century, but so are many other countries.

Don't give a moment's thought about coming to New Zealand. It would seem to you to be like moving to a backward small town in one of the less civilized areas of Kansas or Iowa. We are more or less used to it, and in any case we are stuck with it. Neither of us could make a move now, and we wouldn't know where to go if we could. I can't offer any recommendations, and I agree with you: the world is in a mess. What makes it interesting is seeing what happens next.

Love and good wishes from us both.
Desmond